Albuquerque Mennonite Church
1300 Girard Blvd. NE
Albuquerque, NM 87106

The Limits of Perfection: A Conversation with J. Lawrence Burkholder

Rodney J. Sawatsky
and
Scott Holland
editors

Published by:
Institute of Anabaptist and Mennonite Studies
Conrad Grebel College
Waterloo, Ontario
N2L 3G6

and

Pandora Press
51 Pandora Avenue
Kitchener, Ontario
N2H 3C1

ISBN 0-9698762-2-X
(previously ISBN 0-9697842-0-8)

Printed in Canada on
acid-free paper

Contents

Introduction

Scott Holland

In the spring of 1992 Laurelville Mennonite Church Center in Pennsylvania hosted a theological conference on the thought of J. Lawrence Burkholder. The program, "Conversations with J. Lawrence Burkholder on the Church in Society," brought together Mennonite academics, pastors, church leaders, and lay professionals to explore and critically assess Burkholder's thought and its contribution to past, present, and future proposals for Mennonite and revisionist Anabaptist theology and ethics. This volume was conceived at Laurelville. The quality of intellectual engagement on issues of faith seeking understanding and expression through the diverse communities of church, academy, and society was so high that co-editor Rod Sawatsky and I wanted to extend the discussions and reflections to a larger circle of readers and conversation partners.

The conference planning committee wished to move beyond the hegemony of biblical and historical studies in the Mennonite academy by inviting a theologian whose life and thought has been enriched by the largeness of the world. Weary of uncompromising ideological readings of the Jesus story in an age of stubborn tribalism and increasing sectarian violence, we wanted to hear from a theological thinker who views the spinning, sensuous living world not merely as an *object* for theological description and prophetic critique, but also as a wonderfully complex *source* for creative, disciplined theological revision and construction.

Uneasy with the harsh dualisms between Christ and culture or between the church and the world that are presented in traditional renderings of the Anabaptist vision, the committee wanted to offer conference participants an occasion to think honestly and imaginatively about a faith and ethics capable of leading them to a well-integrated life. As a mentor in this mutual quest, we desired a wise and seasoned theologian who finds both spiritual challenge and human pleasure in the interpenetrating and interdependent realms of ontology and ethics, nature and grace, the private and public, and church and society. We invited J. Lawrence Burkholder in part because we believed the integrity of his life and the richness of his experience, thought, and writing–once rejected as "inadmissible" by powerful Mennonite leaders and thus long neglected by the church–could contribute something significant to our understanding of the Christian life and public responsibility in a fallen yet graced world.

As moderator of the Laurelville event, I encouraged Burkholder to prepare

Scott Holland is a Ph.D. candidate in the Theology Department at Duquesne University in Pittsburgh, Pa.

his presentations in an autobiographical, narrative genre rather than in more formal, academic prose. Knowing of his almost uncanny ability to show up at dramatic historical intersections–he was in Red Square during the failed coup against Boris Yeltsin, in East Germany when the Berlin Wall fell, and in China shortly after the democracy movement was crushed in Tiananmen Square–I invited him to provide narrative glimpses into life as he has seen it, not simply through the safe paper worlds of theological texts and dogmas but through the dangerous and ambiguous worlds of dreams, blood, and bones.

After all, most of his critics who successfully silenced him in the church worked out their theologies of normative Anabaptism and radical Christianity in the comfortable libraries of Heidelberg, Basel, Chicago, or Goshen. Unable to justify existentially a sectarian retreat from worldly responsibility into a utopian theology or community while the world was on fire with war, Burkholder took the Anabaptist tradition seriously, yet saw the limits of perfectionism as a young pilot flying relief missions in India and China. As he surveyed the skies, the brilliant light and the dark, turbulent, haunting clouds, he saw that the place where heaven and earth meet is not as clearly identifiable as his teachers, preachers, and peers had led him to believe. He saw that as one's vision of the world in all its wonder, tragedy, plurality, and ambiguity increases through moving into unfamiliar or unexplored territory, one's ethical and theological horizon must also expand.

Frederick Buechner suggests that at its heart most theology, like most fiction, is essentially autobiography. He writes: "Aquinas, Calvin, Barth, Tillich, working out their systems in their own ways and in their own language, are all telling us the stories of their lives, and if you press them far enough, even at their most cerebral and forbidding, you will find an experience of flesh and blood, a human face smiling or frowning or weeping or covering its eyes before something that happened once."[1] Many theologians are not as honest and self-revealing as Burkholder is about the narrative contexts of their theological programs.

Burkholder's intriguing autobiographical reflections give us a remarkable narrative theology and ethics. Unlike some advocates of narrative theology who present the Christian story like a stone that has fallen from heaven onto the theologian's desk, Burkholder demonstrates how historical circumstance and social location must give rise to serious thought about how classic Christian narratives and doctrines are to be appropriated and understood in the development of personal and social ethics. Such ethics must not avoid the complicated questions as to how love, justice, and power are to embrace, or at least to salute one another.

1 Frederick Buechner, *The Alphabet of Grace* (New York: Harper and Row, 1970), 3.

Burkholder's autobiographical theology is never an exercise in mere self-expression. His narrative is strikingly attentive to the voices and stories of others. Whether allowing us to listen in on the probing questions of gunsmith Jack Woolschlager, showing us the terrified eyes of an elderly Chinese woman as she is forcefully evicted from an airplane, or leading us into conversation with non-Mennonite theologians like Nygren, Tillich, or Niebuhr, he seems to present the encounter with the other as an occasion for self-transcendence. This encounter has the potential of transforming conventional understandings of self, community, and even God as one receives an enlarged self through seeing the largeness of the world.

To fully appreciate the scope of Burkholder's thought one should read his autobiographical essay in conjunction with his more theoretical work. However, one theologian who has known Burkholder for well over thirty years recently confessed that it was only after reading the autobiography that he began to understand the depth, complexity, and importance of Burkholder's theological vision.

Burkholder's spiritual, intellectual, and professional journey has made him painfully aware of the limits of Christian perfectionism and of the necessity of compromise in our broken, de-centered world. He is convinced that the high ethical ideals of Scripture cannot be embodied unambiguously. He has become terribly suspicious of theologies which imply we can impose the so-called pure politics of Jesus upon the often conflicting and competing demands of political, institutional, and social life. He reminds us that in many ways the life of Jesus was not representative of ordinary life, even in its first-century context.

Burkholder believes the existential and theological tension this awareness creates must be addressed honestly and compassionately as Christians seek to bring Christ to bear on the evolving delights and dilemmas of concrete historical existence. The Christian faith calls one to struggle with life's tensions, paradoxes, contradictions, and mysteries. To do less is to trade the Christian birthright for a pot of ideological stew.

The publication of this autobiographical narrative will undoubtedly raise both old and new concerns about Burkholder's critique of perfectionism. Many in our theological tradition fear that his carefully nuanced emphasis on necessary compromise risks reducing the high cost of discipleship as the believer too easily concedes to the ethics of empire. I think not. A close reading of Burkholder may reveal that the cost of Christian discipleship is much higher than some Mennonite theologians and pastors care to admit. Burkholder's program suggests that a departure from sectarian radicalism to more accommodating intellectual systems and lifestyles may not be a mere concession to the demands of empire, but rather a way "to serve Christ by loving the neighbor with greater understanding and effectiveness."[2] We may indeed be called to sacrifice our claims to purity and perfectionism for the love of God, neighbor, and world; for to love the world is to accept responsibility for its history.

When Burkholder first began to test these ideas in the Mennonite Church over thirty years ago, he was searching for conversation partners but found little sympathy for his work. He was told that the questions he had identified as crucial for theological and ethical reflection were not being asked and should not be asked in either the Mennonite Church or the academy. At least in Old Mennonite circles he was quite alone. Even when he was invited back to Goshen College to become its president after many years at Harvard, some have observed that while he was warmly received as an excellent administrator and distinguished churchman, his theology was still not taken very seriously. Happily, all things turn. Today many in the church are finding insight, wisdom, and grace in his writings.

The essays collected in this book were written in response to the autobiography and thus critically engage Burkholder on the themes of his reflections. Three of the essays were delivered as papers at the Laurelville conference (those of Sawatsky, Reimer, and Weaver), as was the response of J.R. Burkholder. The other pieces were collected after the conference.

A wonderfully reckless streak of drama, danger, and adventure runs through Burkholder's life and thought. Julia Kasdorf's "Flying Lesson," a poem/portrait of Burkholder, nicely captures the theologian's restless quest. As Kasdorf recalls a conversation with president Burkholder about her plans to leave Goshen and go to New York City to study and write, she shows us something of the generosity and pastoral sensitivity of the old flyer's heart. Indeed, he tells his story to encourage her to find and follow her own.

Burkholder reports that he is quite happy with Rod Sawatsky's description of him as a "sectarian realist." Sawatsky's article provides a lucid analysis of the careful dialectical movement within Burkholder's theology and ethics as he seeks to find balance between contemporary historical realities and the virtues of his sectarian heritage. Although very interested in the idealistic "oughts" of discipleship, Burkholder's baptism in reality and his understanding of Ernst Troeltsch and the Niebuhr brothers prevent him from denying the often tragic, realistic "is" of the human condition. Living in this tension between the "ought" and the "is," it seems, has opened him to a deep understanding of God's grace. By bringing Burkholder's thought into dialogue with other proposals for Mennonite theology, Sawatsky adds clarity to often misunderstood concepts in

2 J. Lawrence Burkholder, "The Limits of Perfection: Autobiographical Reflections," in this volume, 34.

Burkholder's program such as tragic necessity, compromise, moral dilemmas, social responsibility, perfectionism, and grace.

James Reimer offers a comparative study of three theologians, all of whom came of age during the historical and theological renaissance of Anabaptist idealism: John Howard Yoder, Gordon Kaufman and Lawrence Burkholder. All three thinkers have developed different models for how Mennonites might relate to modern culture. Reimer's comparative approach provides helpful examples of a growing Mennonite theological pluralism.

But Reimer is most interested in classical Christianity and how the Anabaptist-Mennonite tradition has its genealogical origins in the councils, creeds, and confessions of the historic church. Reimer agrees with Burkholder's sociological critique of sectarian perfectionism, and he challenges Mennonites to take a hard look at our self-congratulatory myths of identity and admit that we too make compromises. We too have our identity and being in the historic church, the church of saints and sinners.

Displaying the influences of H.S. Bender's historiography and John Howard Yoder's christology and ecclesiology, J. Denny Weaver's article seeks to develop a Mennonite theology of social responsibility which is quite distinct from the paradigms offered by classical Christendom. According to Weaver the church is called to be radically different from the world, and thus most faithfully and efficiently expresses social responsibility through its redeemed churchly community rather than through the worldly institutions of society. While in agreement with Burkholder's criticism of the withdrawn alternative community proposed by Bender and others, he worries that Burkholder's social ethics risks moving the church dangerously close to "Constantinian Christianity." In contrast to what he sees as the bi-polar options offered by Burkholder, where believers must choose between socially irrelevant, withdrawn moral purity and relevant but compromised activity in the world, Weaver points to a third option: the socially active alternative community.

After commenting on Burkholder's unusual ability to combine lived faith experience and theological reflection in his writing, Ted Koontz's response asks us to consider what we might learn, not merely from Burkholder's extraordinary experiences in China but from his more ordinary years in Goshen, about the problematic nature of all institutions and social structures. After all, Koontz asks, if the same ambiguities, the same problems, and the same dilemmas exist in the church as in other human organizations and structures, as Burkholder argues, what might his thought contribute to a much needed theology of church-related institutions such as colleges, seminaries, hospitals, and mission agencies?

Writing out of his experiences in war-torn Bosnia, Gerald Shenk's response recognizes that the consequences of the moral ambiguities and ethical dilemmas of the late twentieth century were not anticipated in first-century or in sixteenth-century theological agendas. Yet the profound evils of our age–Auschwitz,

Hiroshima, My Lai, Sarajevo–demand a conscientious response. Shenk acknowledges Burkholder's heroic experiments in reluctant responsibility and faithful compromise. Concerning these costly acts of charity and risky moves into the world, Shenk concludes: "The Anabaptists would not be surprised."

Gordon Kaufman, Burkholder's friend and former colleague at Harvard Divinity School, agrees that Mennonites have been too simplistic and naive in their hopes for absolute purity and perfection in a very impure and imperfect world. But Kaufman's concern in his response is to carry this criticism of perfectionism one step further than he thinks Burkholder seems willing to go. Kaufman contends that Burkholder's emphasis on "compromise" leads us to believe that we actually possess some absolute or perfect standard from which we may choose to make compromising moves. Given Burkholder's attention to historicity and the social and cultural contexts of values, Kaufman finds it strange that Burkholder does not question whether the message of Jesus is historically conditioned and thus, in some sense, relative to its time and place. Kaufman's reminder about Jesus' own finitude and historicity must be taken seriously by a new generation of Mennonite theologians who consciously write in the shadow of post-modernism.

Duane Friesen, recognized for his own style of "Christian realism" in ethics, finds much to agree with in Burkholder's dialectical theology. However, he worries that Burkholder's Niebuhrian treatment of Jesus as one who spoke largely to "personal" issues but not "institutional" concerns results in an inadequate christology which gives us a "docetic," disembodied Jesus, unconcerned with the social and political contexts of his time. Friesen's piece gives us another reading of the Jesus narrative–a reading which, following Walter Wink, presents Jesus in an aggressive clash with the "powers that be," since salvation, if it is to be seen in history, is social and not merely personal. Like Burkholder, Friesen has a passion for public responsibility. But his rage for peace and justice is marked by a more optimistic evangelical realism. He presents Jesus Christ as the unambiguous key to *all* reality, and thus the normative standard for *all* institutions, not only the church.

We asked J. Richard Burkholder to sum up the Laurelville conference, so it is fitting for his piece to conclude this collection. He pays tribute to his former philosophy and ethics instructor, who stretched his intellectual horizons at Goshen College, by identifying central themes, questions, and highlights in Burkholder's thought and discussing them within the context of other approaches to theology and ethics, many of which were represented in the intense dialogues and debates at Laurelville. Perhaps most interesting is J.R.'s observation about Burkholder and grace. J.R. notes that during a discussion about discipleship Burkholder said: "If I were writing a theology, I'd begin with soteriology and atonement." Too many Mennonites begin their theology with ethics, not grace. Richard Burkholder suggests that when we open ourselves to God's grace, we can open ourselves to an often hostile world, securely, graciously, and unafraid. Such is the legacy of Lawrence Burkholder.

Gordon Kaufman has recently written that since theology is concerned with ultimate mystery–about which no one can be an *authority*, with certain and final answers–then "the proper model for conceiving it is not the lecture (monologue); nor is it the text (for example, a book); it is, rather, *conversation*."[3] Each human voice, because of its unique place in history, if heard, may open us to a more profound appreciation of life's mysteries. Good theology, therefore, must include a multitude of voices.

It is my hope that this collection of conversations will carry the reader deeper into life's mysteries and inspire courage and curiosity to live life's questions with integrity. As new generations of Mennonites continue to search for more credible models of God and for faithful, responsible ways of being in the world, we are fortunate to have a conversation partner as able and as gracious as J. Lawrence Burkholder, to whom this book is affectionately dedicated.

3 Gordon Kaufman, *In Face of Mystery: A Constructive Theology* (Cambridge: Harvard Press, 1993), 64.

Flying Lesson

Julia Kasdorf

Over a tray of spent plates, I confessed
to the college president my plans to go East,
to New York, which I'd not really seen,
though it seemed the right place
for a sophomore as sullen and restless
as I had become on that merciless
Midwestern plain. He slowly stroked
his thick cup and described the nights
when a theology teacher in Boston, he'd fly
a tiny plane alone out over the ocean,
each time pressing a bit farther into the dark
until the last moment, when he'd turn
toward the coast's bright spine;
how he loved the way the city glittered
beneath him as he glided gracefully toward it,
engine gasping, fuel needle dead
on empty, the way sweat dampened
the back of his neck when he climbed
from the cockpit, giddy. Buttoned up
in my cardigan, willing to lose everything,
I was too young to see generosity
or warning, but now that I'm out here,
his advice comes so clear: fling yourself
farther and a bit farther each time,
but darling, don't drop.

for JLB

Julia Kasdorf is Assistant Professor of Writing at Messiah College, Grantham, Pa. Her book of poetry, *Sleeping Preacher* (University of Pittsburgh Press, 1992), explores the tensions and conflicts that exist between her Mennonite heritage and the invitation to live honestly and passionately in the modern world.

I
The Limits of Perfection: Autobiographical Reflections

The Limits of Perfection: Autobiographical Reflections

J. Lawrence Burkholder

I

I began to think critically and existentially about Christian ethics in the context of what may be considered the most extreme of circumstances in modern times, World War II. At that time I was a young pastor of a small Mennonite congregation in northern New York state, having graduated in 1942 from the Lutheran Theological Seminary at Gettysburg, Pennsylvania. Mennonites had no seminary at that time.

During the War, I assisted young conscientious objectors to receive the 1-W draft classification. I was called before a local draft board to witness to the sincerity of Mennonite and Amish draftees. This led to public interpretations of the Mennonite position on war in a predominantly Catholic rural community. I chose simply to quote appropriate verses of Scripture, and I appealed to the life and teachings of Jesus as reflected especially in the Sermon on the Mount. The draft board treated my witness respectfully.

However, the chairman of the board, a local gunsmith, argued the case for Christian participation in war from what I later discovered was the classical doctrine of the "just war." He argued that Hitler and Tojo were diabolical and that their victory over the Allies would bring Western civilization to an end. None of us was aware at that time of some six million Jews who were being exterminated, but I had to agree that a victory by totalitarian powers would constitute an unparalleled tragedy. The board chairman personalized his attack by claiming that if Hitler were to prevail, I would be responsible for the death of many people and the end of humane institutions and just orders.

I responded to his criticism with simple logic about the relative insignificance of a single person in relation to such a great historical development as World War II. But he insisted that while I might not be guilty for having set the world afire, I was obligated to help, as any neighbor would be, to put it out. And so I struggled with a gnawing sense of guilt for my negligence. Even though pacifism, as held by a small minority, would seem relatively innocuous given the enormity of the historical crisis, could the Mennonite position unwittingly contribute to the forces of darkness? Furthermore, I was impressed with the irony that Mennonites who, while stemming from a tradition of martyrdom,

J. Lawrence Burkholder taught at Harvard Divinity School and is retired from the presidency of Goshen College in Goshen, Indiana.

sacrificed no more than the risk of social involvement in mental hospitals at a time when many Catholics, Presbyterians, and others, who made no claims to Christian heroism, left home and family only to return in body bags.

I was shaken those days by the demonic character of organized evil as represented by totalitarian aggression. My pacifism was basically Mennonite. It made provision for an evil world out there, however, without my being of it or responsible for it. But, ironically, while at Gettysburg, a Lutheran seminary, I came under the influence of modern liberal pacifism with its optimistic view of human nature and especially the assumption that pacifism was prudent as well as Christian. I assumed that to turn the other cheek would shame the enemy into goodness. But World War II dashed such naive pacifist optimism. Though a registered but deferred conscientious objector, I had to admit that Hitler was utterly evil and must be stopped by somebody, somehow. Hence, while continuing to preach against war in general, I found it difficult to preach against this war in particular. In fact I found myself hoping that the Allies would prevail. My conscience was troubled, and I was uncertain about what to do as a deferred conscientious objector.

In one of our private discussions, Jack Woolschlager, the gunsmith of German background, proposed that my theology of the Sermon on the Mount was irresponsible and implicitly anarchistic, and as such, dangerous. The Sermon on the Mount, he claimed, makes inadequate provision, if any, for the restraint of evil. After all, security is an essential support of life, along with food, shelter, water, and air. Those who would "love the enemy" in principle, i.e., in any and all circumstances, expose their neighbors in a manner analogous to allowing them to starve and freeze to death unassisted. To forgive seventy times seven is to turn criminals loose to prey on the weak. Though claiming to be a Christian, Woolschlager insisted that the ethic of Jesus had to be counter-balanced by the ethic of the Old Testament. In that way the anarchism of love would be contained and limited by the "law of God," thereby providing the basis for an ordered society. Somehow I had not thought of myself as an anarchist, and yet I had made no theological provision for the use of lethal force, not even in the Schleitheim sense of separation of roles and responsibilities. I had really never thought systematically about social ethics.

We also discussed whether the war issue should turn ultimately on moral or religious considerations or on both. We agreed that to kill in war and not to kill in war could be problematic when seen strictly from a moral point of view. Killing for the sake of the innocent is at least morally ambiguous. Even Woolschlager acknowledged that. I insisted that to kill for the sake of the innocent is more morally abhorrent than not to kill at all. But he argued that to kill a few people in order to protect many people had the moral advantage. In the end, we rather agreed that killing in a just war could not be settled by placing the issue on the scales of morality alone. It could be settled finally, if at all, on a "religious" level where one's conscience would be moved by one's understanding of the will of God. Similarly, we agreed that the issue could not be settled by always doing the "loving thing." The question was, what is the loving thing to do in the presence of Hitler? Even so, to admit to myself that pacifism may be morally problematic, though preferable, seemed to place me at odds with the traditional Mennonite consciousness of unambiguous righteousness. At one point in our conversation I raised the theoretical question as to whether "the moral thing" and "the right thing" were the same, the right thing being that which corresponds to God's will. Can it be wrong to do the moral thing? Conversely, can it be right to do the immoral thing? Are God's will and morality of the same order, or do they represent different realities, sometimes identical in content and sometimes not, depending upon the situation?

As best as I can remember our conversations, Woolschlager took the position that God transcends the moral order. The moral order is a human, natural, and changeable creation of culture. Morality is of "our own making,"a rather amazing observation for a man of his circumstance and sort. Norms grounded in the moral order may help to define normal daily behavior. As a general rule, morality and God's will coincide, he said, but there are exceptional times and circumstances when the Almighty wills what is normally considered immoral for the sake of "something down the road." We must be immoral by human standards to be ethical by God's "exceptional standards." We must kill for the sake of love as any policeman may be required to do, however regretfully. After shooting a violent criminal, a policeman would return to his normal duties, subject to normal standards.

Woolschlager cited the conquest of Canaan as biblical proof that under exceptional circumstances God may even order the wholesale extermination of men, women, and children. Therefore, if God has indeed commanded conquest in ancient times, is it not reasonable that God may approve the defense of Western nations against the very incarnation of evil in modern times?

As a young, idealistic product of Mennonite life and indoctrination, I had never before run into that kind of thinking. It was shocking. It appeared to me to be logically contradictory or at best paradoxical. As a young rationalist for whom consistency was tantamount to cleanliness, I could not tolerate the irrational, the ambiguous. Woolschlager's position seemed to imply divine caprice, and it threatened to separate God from the moral order. I thus made the point that maybe the trans-moral exception that he talked about could take an exactly opposite form, namely love for the enemy. In time of war, love for the enemy would at least be more exceptional than to go to war. But in that context, my argument was more impressive as a debating point than as serious justification for pacifism.

This brought us into the court of biblical interpretation. Neither of us were prepared for a hermeneutical debate since neither of us knew much about the subject. Woolschlager's layman's theology seemed to be located primarily in the Old Testament. By contrast, I had such a distaste for certain conceptions of God in the Old Testament that I was virtually a Marcion, as were many traditional Mennonites at that time.

What I found especially engaging was Woolschlager's honest and rigorous definition of the problem. The issue was not one of political alternatives or of nice questions about whether it is ever right to use force, but of whether it is right under the most extreme conditions for Christians to kill as an act of love for the sake of others.

Actually, my feelings toward participation in war were not entirely determined by scriptural authority and discipleship faith. I was certainly no biblicist in the legalistic sense; I just could not imagine killing another human being. My imagination would not allow me to depersonalize war as some were accustomed to do, and I could not distance myself by linguistic sleight-of-hand from the horrors of bombing "installations" and shooting down "airplanes." I was compelled to think about innocent people burned alive and mowed down in crossfire. To me the issue of war was an emotional one. Quite apart from considerations of Christian ethics, I simply did not have the courage, fortitude, guts, patriotism, or whatever it takes to kill other people.

My sensitivity extended back to childhood when, for example, I was deeply moved by some "war books" which were closeted at my grandmother's house. These histories of the Spanish-American War included graphic pictures of hand-to-hand combat in which even women and children were bayoneted. At a county fair the U.S. Army displayed a small military tank that I could not touch–as if it were an eerie ark of evil. From my earliest recollections, pacifism was intensely personal and heartfelt.

But the same moral reflections that enabled me to help conscientious objectors to find alternative service also evoked a sense of responsibility for the victims of totalitarian aggression in Europe and Asia. I could not separate myself from the crisis of the times, even as a pastor of a small rural Mennonite church. To be sure, I was deferred from the draft as a minister. But when the bells of the Croghan village Catholic Church tolled, announcing the death of local Catholic youth, I was troubled.

World War II brought to me for the first time the reality of moral conflict. I had always assumed that moral obligation implied simple, unilateral, black and white, undialectical alternatives of a decidedly unambiguous character. I had assumed that uncompromising moral obligation implied perfect moral freedom. I believed that the only moral impediments were volitional in nature–possibly deceptive but certainly not "necessary." Moral failure was always a failure of will. Didn't the Apostle Paul teach that, "No temptation has overtaken you that is not common to man. God is faithful and he will not let you be tempted beyond your strength, but with temptation will also provide the way of escape, that you may be able to endure it" (1 Cor. 10:13)? I had assumed that a "way of escape" would be available if we would only look for it intelligently, repentantly, patiently, and persistently. After all, is this not a moral universe?

Nothing in my Mennonite background had prepared me to make any but unambiguous choices. Thus, World War II threatened my view of the universe as a creation of God in support of moral perfection. But the choice of either killing other human beings or letting Hitler kill with abandon seemed to present a dilemma of such depth and proportions that I felt that I had to rethink my theology, and especially my understanding of the nature of moral obligation.

Oddly enough, I felt that both those who fight to save Western institutions and those who refuse to fight for "righteousness's sake" are caught in the same dilemma, and both are in need of forgiveness. I could not assign clean hands to either soldiers or pacifists. Both need the grace of God. In this respect, my experience was not typically Mennonite. For if there are on record Mennonites seeking to be forgiven for having gone to Civilian Public Service camps, I have not found them. I suppose that I was at that time a kind of vocational pacifist, though I did not know the term. At any rate, I chose not to dissuade my Catholic and mainline church neighbors from supporting the war. So Woolschlager and I parted.

What Woolschlager took away from our discussions was the question of whether one who kills in a war such as World War II has committed a horrible sin in need of "justification," or whether killing in World War II on the side of the Allies is righteous because God wills it and therefore does not need to be justified. He leaned toward the latter. I came down on the former.

II

Eventually, the tension between pacifism to which my wife Harriet and I were committed and the case for military protection of innocent people and democratic values became unbearable. We simply could not live out the war in the relative tranquility of the pastorate in northern New York state. To be sure, we were living simply: I worked five days a week at a sawmill to make ends meet while doing pastoral work on marginal time. We received little support from our loving Amish-minded congregation, and we were relatively poor as many young pastors were in those days. But the stakes were high, and we agreed that an honorable and reasonable Christian response to the immensity of the times would have to be extreme. What could we do as disciples of Jesus Christ which would constitute something of a moral alternative, if not a moral equivalent, (these are not necessarily the same) to participation in armed struggle against the evils of Nazism and Japanese expansionism?

The answer seemed to come in the summer of 1944, when I read a news bulletin in *The New York Times* by Theodore White, the famous reporter who described, in most graphic and heartrending language, starvation and cannibalism in Honan Province, China. There the war between China and Japan was being complicated by civil strife between the Nationalist and Communist armies. As if by Providence, about that time the Mennonite Central Committee announced its intention to start a relief program in China, and the Mennonite Board of Missions decided to search for a mission somewhere in China. It was hard to get to that country then since it was necessary to enter by the back door over the Hump from India. I had no previous inclinations toward China; I knew virtually nothing about Chinese culture and not a word of Chinese language. However, I had youthful memories of my father's idealization of Herbert Hoover as a relief administrator in Europe following World War I, and as a young pilot, I indulged in romantic images of Lindbergh who had flown supplies in China during the Yellow River floods of the 1930s. The prospect of helping to feed and clothe starving and freezing people in such a distant, strange, and exotic land as China appealed to my need for an honorable Christian alternative to war which would include a measure of drama, danger, adventure, and heroic sacrifice. So I volunteered and was commissioned to go to China for a two to four-year term for the Elkhart Mission Board, but under the administration of MCC. My assignment was somewhat ambiguous given the uncertainties of war, but it included locating a place for a mission in China. (The General Conference Mennonite Church had at that time an established China mission of many years.)

That Harriet and I and our two little children could be separated up to four years, presuming that all went well, was contemplated as a painful but not unreasonable sacrifice in light of Christ's teaching about the relative claims of the natural family and the call to discipleship (Mark 3:31-35). Further, the risk that we would take, though considerable, seemed not to exceed that of those who went to war.

When on the dock in Baltimore waiting to board the "Benjamin Pixato," a liberty ship laden with military hardware for its maiden voyage, I met by accident a young black Merchant Marine officer who was under orders to sail unescorted to the northern Russian city of Murmansk. This assignment would take him into a North Atlantic route above the Arctic Circle where eight out of ten allied merchant ships on similar courses were being destroyed by German U-boat submarines. To make it in winter through those terrible waters to Russia and to return safely was a matter of extremely low probability. Were the freighter torpedoed, the crew would either go down with it or freeze to death in life boats. This black officer, with a wife and four children in Washington, was looking at his probable death, since he saw no escape. "If there were only a way out," he said plaintively. I pitied him and counted myself fortunate to enjoy a higher probability of survival across the Atlantic Ocean to Gibraltar in convoy, and then unescorted to Calcutta through the Suez and the Indian Ocean.

The China years that followed became the crucible for my ethical thinking. I had never had a course in ethics; my ethics came directly out of the encounter between Mennonite radical idealism and reality. I had imbibed a lot of Mennonite attitudes and presuppositions as they took the form of heroic discipleship and nonresistance. In those days, even before Guy Hershberger's *War, Peace, and Nonresistance*,[1] separatistic nonresistance was implicit if not well articulated as the key to Mennonite life. It implied nonparticipation in the give-and-take of social conflict. Mennonites made no positive theological sense of justice, power, and arbitration in those days. Voting was discouraged, though not prohibited. Purity and obeying church rules and regulations dominated all other religious considerations. Pacifism was interpreted as avoidance of war, not making peace. Membership in labor unions was discouraged, if not forbidden. Even defensive litigation was disallowed. The "unequal yoke" was sometimes carried so far as to forbid membership in local voluntary fire departments as well as business partnerships with "unbelievers." Marriage outside the Mennonite church was forbidden and divorce was almost unheard of. A two-kingdom theology of separation from the world was reinforced with strong discipline. The Lancaster Conference went so far as to excommunicate some of my relatives for having life insurance, so strict was the discipline and so literal the interpretation of Jesus' ethics of filial trust (Matt. 6:19). The church insisted that the logic of nonresistance was separation from the social order. To be in the world without being of the world was considered possible and necessary through deliberate nonconformity. If total separation were impossible, lines were nevertheless drawn that would express concretely an alternative way of life. And so I carried to India and China a deeply ingrained nonconformist consciousness with which I was theologically and emotionally in agreement, except for some of the so-called "cultural" regulations, such as plain coats and the prescribed length of women's sleeves.

But during the wartime crossing of the Atlantic in a naval convoy of some eighty ships, aboard a freighter whose deck was laden with explosives and other military ordnance, I discovered some things about myself. I discovered that despite my faith and youthful idealism, I too was human. I was as vulnerable to fear as were cursing sailors. The possibility of being sunk was real, especially as our ship, having left the convoy at Gibraltar, hugged the North African coast unescorted and finally sailed up and down the eastern coast of India for nearly a week waiting for its turn to enter the Hooghly River to Calcutta. Our freighter was a sitting duck for Japanese submarines operating in those waters. A liberty ship nearby was torpedoed, and lifeboats were machine-gunned. We slept, if at all, with life jackets on, ready to go over the side. In retrospect, that I should have been frightened is quite understandable, but it was a problem to me then. Shouldn't committed disciples transcend fears of death (Matt.10:28)? Shouldn't conscientious objectors transcend ordinary human frailties, as uncompromising nonresistance would seem to imply? Whether I was more fearful than my MCC companions, Clayton Beyler and Ralph Kaufman, I don't

1 Guy F. Hershberger, *War, Peace, and Nonresistance* (Scottdale, Pa.: Herald Press, 1946).

know. We didn't talk about our inner feelings very much.

On board was a radio operator who seemed to have no fear of anything. He was not of the defiant, hell-raising sort like the Flying Tigers with whom I later flew on relief missions in China. He was a quiet, emotionless person, impassive and almost mechanical in his movements, and as rational as a skillful mathematician, which indeed he was. We discussed the statistical probabilities of being struck by all kinds of ordnances. He had it all figured out, but he placed his statistics within a larger framework of Stoic fatalism. "Don't worry," he said, "If a torpedo has your name on it, you will go down with us all." What comfort! So I pondered faith in God over against chance and naturalistic determinism. I found no rational basis upon which to make such an ultimate choice, and thus I questioned which alternative would be most comforting, given the sort of beings humans are.

If the year spent in Bengal was lonely and my fragility all too evident to me, if not to others, I learned in retrospect much about life and the meaning of Christian ethics. In particular, I noticed a distinct difference between love in its simple purity and in its social and organizational refraction. By pure love I mean disinterested love, unmixed with anticipated rewards, reciprocations, mutual gratification, and preferences based upon merit. I noticed that the bureaucratic administration of social services through organized personnel, money, and goods brought their rewards. I look back upon that year with satisfaction that a considerable number of people would have starved to death had no one representing MCC and the Mennonite Board of Missions been there. But what I recall most vividly are those instances when it was my privilege to serve people directly and apart from any thought of achievement, reputation, or reciprocation–that is, when I was by direct analogy a Good Samaritan expressing in pure simplicity what I later found Anders Nygren to identify as *agape* love.[2]

One example occurred on an afternoon when I was examining a relief program in the Ganges delta some distance from Calcutta. A little girl, possibly eight years old, took my hand–an audacious act in itself, given Indian practices–and led me to her bamboo hut. In the darkness she showed me her widowed mother, a little woman of skin and bones lying in filthy rags in the corner, too weak to speak. On her head was a large ulcer exposing most of her skull, maggots having devoured her flesh. The odor was unbearable. No medical help was available in those parts, and I could only hope that she would die. I gave the little girl some money and left. That was all I could do, it seemed. But I found no peace, and the next morning I returned to the hut, finding the woman still alive. I administered to her some sulfa powder of the kind that all of us carried in those days. To my surprise she improved day by day and was able

2 Anders Nygren, *Agape and Eros* (London: SPCK, 1953), 14.

to sit up by the time I left the community.

I feel apologetic for recalling this incident with particular satisfaction. To have helped a woman in such a manner is nothing spectacular or particularly heroic in itself. Medical people save lives routinely. Why do I recall this incident, while letting the daily administration of duties having greater effectiveness recede into the dim past?

I believe that the joy of this particular act of kindness was unique because of its agapaic character. It was voluntary, personal, direct, discrete, unreciprocating love unmixed by self-regarding motivations. That not all of life moves on this level is a fact of considerable significance for a theory of ethics. Unfortunately, most of our "loving" is not of this sort. Most loving relationships are mutual, as are church life, friendship, business, and civil relationships of all sorts at their best. But *agape*, though sometimes leading to community, transcends communal relationships. Hence Jesus reminds us that "If you love those who love you, what reward will you get? Are not the tax collectors doing that . . . ? Be perfect, (i.e., indiscriminate) therefore, as your heavenly father is perfect" (Matt. 5:46-48).

What I learned in India some years before I became aware that New Testament scholars assigned unique ethical significance to *agape* was that all human relationships must be judged by their approximation to *agape*, just as the relative must be measured by its relation to the absolute, the temporal to the eternal, and the partial to the complete. *Agape* transcends ordinary relationships, especially when individuals as well as collectives assert themselves in the ordinary struggle for existence. That is why death on the cross is the perfect symbol of absolute love. An important implication of the absoluteness of *agape* is that *agape* love cannot be structured unambiguously, for structure itself generally includes self-regarding implications, defenses, safeguards, lines of exclusion, and sanctions.

During my experience as a relief administrator, whether for MCC or Church World Service or for the United Nations, protective devices, distribution policies, arbitrated salary scales, insurance claims, retirement plans, and contractual agreements, not to speak of government regulations, forced *agape* to be exceptional and to occupy a realm above the operational presumptions of day-to-day activities. Life, especially collective life, could not be run by *agape* alone. *Agape* may, however, serve as an ideal point of reference. It may invade the give-and-take of power structures under ad hoc circumstances but not on a continuous basis. *Agape* punctuates, but does not constitute, organized life.

My fascination with *agape* love antedates my knowledge of it as a New Testament concept. It was expressed by my mother during the depression of the 1930s when she ministered voluntarily to the needs of poor neighbors. I recall coming home from school on numerous occasions, almost as a rule it seems, to find battered women sitting in our kitchen recounting their troubles. She listened daily to horror stories about drunken husbands, wayward children, and being out of food. Many jars of canned meat and vegetables were removed from our pantry and given to those poor women and their children. My mother was concerned about social diseases, so the chairs upon which these women sat were routinely placed outside to air off after they left. So often she would say during a cold winter evening, "I pity the poor people." But she was no bleeding heart and she seldom verbalized her faith–seldom, if ever, referring to her generosity as religiously grounded. She did not, so far as I remember, "witness" to the poor. Her generosity seemed to be natural and spontaneous, as if that is how life is lived.

Obviously, my mother was a deeply committed Christian. She taught Sunday school and dressed plainly. But the connection between her love for others and her faith had to be inferred from the quality of her acts and her demeanor–not from conscious self-disclosure. Only after receiving a theological education did I associate her character and acts of love with what the New Testament was about–so completely and unconsciously did she internalize the spirit of Christ. But even as a child, I could tell that she was different from most people. With my mother, it was a case of pure love for those whose only reciprocation was their attendance at her funeral. Her love transcended the mutuality of friendship and communal fellowship. "For if you love those who love you, what thanks have you?" is Christ's warning against those who would assign to all sorts of mutual associations, including religious organizations, the uniqueness of *agape*. Organizations like koinonia groups, mutual aid, and relief administrations are bound to draw lines of exclusion and enjoy the benefits of reciprocation. *Agape* love judges all other modes and manifestations of love. My experience in India seemed to reinforce my faith that such love is an historical possibility but is at best an occasional one, since it cannot be structured without contradiction.

I would add parenthetically that *agape* is not necessarily Christian simply because it is the name used for love in the New Testament. *Agape* is to be thought of as a relationship of a particular kind and not considered in essentialist terms as some sort of heavenly substance emanating from God. As such, it may be embodied by advocates of other religions or by those who profess no religion at all.

One of the surprises of my life in those days was to encounter a wealthy Hindu merchant who responded to the Bengal famine by giving his entire estate to the poor. He organized a work project for starving people. The fact that the work consisted of making clay idols seemed to me, a Christian, more interesting than significant so far as his generosity was concerned.

By the time I got to China one year later, I had had some experience as an administrator of relief. This eventually led to my becoming director of the American Advisory Committee representing Church World Service, with headquarters in Shanghai. Since the Committee accepted responsibility for the importation of supplies for major Protestant denominations whose missionaries were returning by the hundreds and thousands to China (including Harriet and our children), the war having ended, I became involved in practical dealings with customs, insurance agencies, transportation firms, office staff, inter-religious organizations, currency exchanges, and government agencies.

The moral significance of all this was that I continued to learn about the difference between the ethics of personal relations and corporate responsibilities. I learned that to head an organization which participated in a web of interacting corporate, often competing, interests both enhanced and limited the possibility of loving service. Responsibilities of a corporate nature were necessarily conditioned by the complexity of the situation. Discriminating judgments had to be made emanating from written contracts, legal obligations, and a sense of fairness. The language of rights, due process, ownership, and claims tended to replace spontaneous responses to need. And the larger the operation, the more impersonal and bureaucratic relationships became. Soon I came to see myself as an administrator and business executive rather than as a Good Samaritan. Certainly, people were being helped, but within limits determined by "the nature of things." The joy of moral freedom, the creative spontaneity, the unpredictability of the Spirit, and the possibility of miracle such as characterized the ministry of Jesus were reduced to stereotypical processes, bureaucratic procedures, and legal necessities. Of course, bureaucracy enhanced effectiveness when measured by numbers of people impacted. Effectiveness is terribly important. But what could be considered distinctly and uniquely Christian, namely the freedom to respond with uncircumscribed, unbridled grace, was severely reduced, if not lost.

Further, I found myself in a position of power–though, to be sure, not the power of a top industrialist. The American Advisory Committee was a relatively small organization, though national in the scope of its operations. But I recall endorsing a check from the United China Relief fund for one million dollars–a tremendous amount of money at that time. To operate at the head of a vertically organized staff presented me with unanticipated responsibilities for the welfare of employees and for negotiating from a position of power with "coolie" unions and Chinese authorities. To make decisions about who shall be given this or that and who shall not receive the same bothered this idealist of less than thirty years of age. In the most severe situations of starvation, decisions had to be made that meant that some would live and others would die. It appeared to me that *agape* love and power and complexity were in tension, if not in conflict.

I recall the first employee I fired. It was a crisis because my ethics called for infinite forgiveness, which appeared to be an implication of Jesus' command to forgive seventy times seven. A dishonest employee was caught stealing relief materials. After receiving a confession from him, I allowed him to remain on the job. Soon, however, the Shanghai police caught him stealing as before. He would have been jailed had I not interceded. After his being caught the third time, the American Advisory Committee, consisting mostly of missionaries and Chinese Christians of some distinction, insisted that he be fired. They claimed that I had no right to inject my personal Mennonite ethics into an inter-denominational organization. After all, the employee was not stealing from the director, they said, but from all organizations associated with Church World Service. So I fired him. But I learned something about the power and the moral limits of corporate administration. Something in me died in the process.

My radical idealism was especially shocked on an occasion during the evacuation of Shenyang, then called Mukden, Manchuria. The city was falling to the Communists. Part of it was on fire. I was the co-pilot of one of General Claire Chennault's DC-3s. For five days we had flown planeloads of refugees to Peking, returning with food for the people left in that ghost city. But on the last day of evacuations, after the U.S. Consul's plane left, signaling the end, refugees panicked. Some nearly hysterical Chinese crowded into the plane and even on to the wings. The captain, a Flying Tiger, and I lost control of the situation. He dared not even start the engines. The ex-marine pilot ordered me to clear the cabin to a take-off load level. I tried to do so by persuasion, but the people would not budge. At that point the pilot handed me his pistol with which to force evacuation. This I could not do, so he held the gun at the heads of the Chinese while I literally pushed them out. One person whom I removed forcibly was an old Chinese woman with bound feet. I will never forget her expression of fright and despair. She became separated from her husband who remained on the plane, presumably never to see her again. We finally got off the ground, dangerously overloaded, saving ourselves and some thirty-five people. But I found myself having used physical force, along with another person who wielded a gun which he would probably have used if necessary. My innocence was no more. I felt that I was no longer a Mennonite in practice, though maybe at heart–if such a condition is not an Anabaptist-Mennonite contradiction. I lost the "good conscience" about which my former teacher, Harold Bender, talked about so much. Somehow I could accept physical suffering as an implication of discipleship, but I had not been prepared for "tragic necessity."

From then on I could no longer deny the existence of an authentic moral dilemma. I had found it necessary to use force against some so that others could be "saved"–classic reasoning for the "just war." Following this incident I reflected about the structure of the ethical situation. Nonresistance was a principle which could and presumably should always apply when one's personal interests alone were concerned. But what should be done when the welfare of other people was concerned? Before going to China, I had never addressed that question existentially. Harriet and I had anticipated imaginatively a situation involving the attack of a personal assailant. We had decided not to resist, if God were to give us that measure of strength. We decided never to defend each other, at least not by lethal force. But we could not resolve the issue if our small children's lives were concerned, or the lives of our unbelieving neighbors. From the standpoint of "Kingdom ethics," it seemed more imperative to save infants and unbelievers than those who had come to terms with suffering and death through faith.

I was also faced with the problem of how to eat and sleep while others were dying of starvation and cold. That winter of 1946, Shanghai was terribly cold and damp. I lived in an unheated apartment there before Harriet and the children arrived. I had shelter and enough to eat, even though the nutritional value of the food was deficient. But at the entrance to the apartment were homeless refugees. Every evening I stepped over a young Chinese woman with two small children as I came home from the office. I could not take it any longer, so I invited the woman to sleep in the hallway of the apartment, whereupon I got into trouble with the neighbors about "giving relief from the apartment." Such a precedent would lead to a run on the entire apartment complex, so I relented, but with a heavy conscience. It led to questions that any relief worker faces, and indeed, anyone who has poor neighbors. Am I justified from a Christian point of view to live better than the most deprived? This problem is classic.

On December 1947, my involvement in China took a new turn. I was invited to become the Director of the National Clearing Committee, a small quasi-public organization of the United Nations with offices in Shanghai. This committee was organized to transfer title of relief supplies, mostly U.S. Army and Navy war surplus from the South East Asia command, that were scattered throughout China. The recipients were the Bureau of Social Affairs of the Nationalist Government of Chiang Kai-shek, various Communist organizations such as the China Relief Fund, a Communist front, represented by Madame Sun Yat-sen, and the voluntary agencies of which Church World Service was the agent, plus a rather mysterious contingent of shadowy figures representing the Communist army who showed up clandestinely here and there. The project was completed in one year, just prior to our being evacuated from Shanghai by the U.S. Navy.

With an office and staff on the third floor of the Chin Chiang bank building on the Bund, with Nationalist representatives on the second floor and a furtive band of Communists on the ground floor, I learned firsthand something about the meaning of the public sphere and responsibility within a political context. It turned out to be the most exciting, most productive, and most satisfying years of my life, and yet I was shocked by the realities of political policy formation and power. I learned that the political realm could offer an avenue for delivering a lot of this world's goods to alleviate suffering. Thousands upon thousands of cases of foodstuffs, complete mobile hospitals, British textiles and "detasseled" uniforms, Navy landing crafts, crashed airplanes, fire fighting equipment, river boats, cots, blankets, and weather stations were to be given away according to policies worked out in New York and interpreted by UNRRA and Chinese lawyers.

Many of the materials that were to be distributed were on inventory lists only. Amid the confusion of civil war, referred to those days euphemistically as an "incident," it was impossible for the Committee to see what it was supposed to be working with. Confusion enhanced the drama and sometimes provided an excuse for inefficiency. Those were far from normal times.

But barely a day had passed in office when I recognized a vast difference between service in the private sector and responsibility within the political realm. A most obvious change concerned the role of policy as defined by law. Written policies were part of the work environment to an extent that I had not imagined before. When I left Akron for China in 1944, I had a general idea about what relief workers were supposed to do. If I remember correctly, there were no written instructions except some having to do with personal, moral, and spiritual expectations. But the U.N. defined what should be done through formal policies and legal agreements. Law defined what to do and how to go about it; it designated channels and determined limits. A U.N. administrator could question policies, but s/he had to function within them until they were revised or rescinded.

My response to policies set in advance was positive and negative. Policies were intended to enable the Committee to get the job done well, and by and large, they worked. The Committee distributed a lot of goods as efficiently as the circumstances of political chaos and a civil war would permit.

But I felt a vast difference between personal service and political responsibility, in the sense that policies based upon and defined by law tended to limit one's moral freedom. When the Nationalist or Communist army representatives requested something, we could not respond on the basis of impulse, personal feelings, sympathies or rational sense of justice, and certainly not on the basis of scriptural admonition. We had to respond first and sometimes entirely by reference to UNRRA policies, which usually made considerable moral sense and were at least intended to be fair. But there were times when policies and moral possibilities seemed to conflict. Many times I felt that alternatives were needlessly limited by the set-up. A sense of justice drew me to allocate goods to the parties in greatest need and in accordance with principles of efficiency.

UNRRA policies could not anticipate all eventualities. Sometimes we had to say "no" to the most deserving. I often thought about the parable of the ninety and nine. Policies were not designed for the poor lost lamb but rather for the many sheep. What I searched for during my year with UNRRA was a way to meet the needs of the average Chinese (multitudes) within certain categories and, at the same time, the needs of individuals whose circumstances might take an infinite number of unanticipated forms. I was under the impression that Jesus championed in particular the person who, for whatever reason, fell between the cracks and was lost. Throughout my relief experience I accepted as a goal meeting the needs of those for whom the system made no provision. I was only partially successful. In fact, I saw the demands of uniqueness (the one) and the demands of the generic (the many) to be in tension. Political reality seemed better prepared to meet the latter than the former. Insofar as I was compelled to prefer the many to the one, I sometimes felt sad and guilty even though one could do nothing about it. One could bend policy only so far and get away with it. I learned that the administration of anything large-scale may have the compelling advantage of impacting most people for good, but it will let other people go untouched who especially need help. If the test of Jesus' ethic is to meet the exceptional needs of the exceptional, then to that extent my administration, which by ordinary standards was reasonably successful, was to fail.

During my UNRRA year, I worked closely with a legal advisor, a Bronx Jew named Mary Palevski. She was a tough person with a voice like an elephant's roar, an absolutely honest, procedure-oriented, strict constructionist. I was people-oriented, "soft, sentimental, and too loving," she said. We traveled together in a chartered C-46 transport plane to eight provinces in order to allocate and transfer possession of residual supplies to the Nationalists, the churches, and the Communists. She taught me the ways of the world so far as the exercise of power is concerned. Her New York Jewish background and my Lancaster County Mennonite background appeared in contrast as she insisted that responsible administration included a significant component of fighting for rights, principles, honor, dignity, and power.

I was shocked by the clash of national egos between the Nationalist and Communist representatives, the back door intrigues and ingratiating ploys, the plain dishonesty and veiled threats. I found that most people in the "world" were complex, though in general they were responsible and even likeable as individuals. I got along well on a personal basis with both Nationalist and Communist representatives. Sometimes I felt like a trusted mediator when their attitudes toward each other reflected reality–that their armies were at war. When they faced off in competition around the "negotiation table" to make their case for this or that surplus river boat or warehouse laden with Australian blankets, they became different people. They became uncompromising as representatives for their institutional and partisan egos. They demanded their rights with virtually no recognition of the just claims of the other party. No common ground for the definition and authority of justice was acknowledged. It was dog-eat-dog.

As a nonresistant Mennonite, I was initially shocked only to be reminded by Mary Palevski and Arthur Klein, an UNRRA bureaucrat, that as a representative of the United Nations I too had a corporate power to represent as well. I saw no definitive answer to the question of who gets what beyond the guidelines of the UN mandate. Usually negotiations ended in a compromise with which no one would admit satisfaction. Probably it was unreasonable to expect representatives of warring governments could subordinate collective interests to some sort of abstract justice. Nothing seemed simple those days–not even giving things away!

I became a "divider." Higher-ups ultimately bore responsibility for the work of the commission, but for all practical purposes, decisions had to be made on administrative levels, and that meant we had to make effective decisions on the spot and be prepared to defend them. Soon my self-image came to reflect the duality of personal Mennonite introspection on the one hand and official external assertive power on the other hand. With such differences I began to see the possibilities and limits in both. In general I came to associate the private sphere with spontaneity, compassion, sacrifice, and perfectionistic possibilities, and the public sphere with social effectiveness. Gradually, "to be good" and "to get something done" came into tension if not outright conflict.

What I struggled with especially was the Christian use of power. It was not simply a question of the inevitability of power but the exercise of power in competition with other powers. During that year of experience, often over my head administratively and certainly beyond my philosophical and theological understanding, I found that I had to exercise power over others. "Enabling" power I could accept, but to dominate and counter-balance power with power gave me many a problem.

In my worse or better moments, depending upon one's interpretation, I came to see not giving as taking away. Yet how could one do differently under the conditions of finite resources? To say no to less deserving individuals and organizations was a problem to this very sensitive young idealist. I recalled that when Jesus ran out of resources, he miraculously increased the bread and fishes. This I could not do. Indeed I came to doubt the practical application of the biblical ethic of *agape* love, since the application of love in Jesus' life seemed to presuppose the transcendence of natural limits. I pondered the relations not only of love to justice but of love to power. It is easy to say that power in the abstract is neither good nor bad, but the real question concerns power in its concrete manifestations. In general, I used power for good ends by means that helped some but sometimes hurt others. The use of power implied in ownership, vertical structures, and competitive purposes seemed to be inherently ambiguous.

Most problems of power had to do with the intricacies of distribution in a complex, competitive, and often confusing situation. Sometimes we assigned ownership to goods that were located one day within Nationalist-held territory only to find that the Communists had taken that territory the next day. What was especially disturbing to me was deliberate falsification of information. The Nanking government was especially corrupt, so much so that it was necessary to call for sanctions, however ineffective. But legal processes would frequently mean that food would spoil or get lost. As well, to bring sanctions against the Nationalists was politically unpopular with American political interests at that time. Hence, pressure to keep quiet.

The Communists were generally more honest than the Nationalists, it seemed, but also more insistent upon their share of goods. I am quite sure that they got their share, but they were forever complaining to Madame Sun Yat-sen, patron saint of the China Relief Fund. A German woman married to a Chinese man complained bitterly and accusingly to me on behalf of CLARA, a Communist relief organization in support of a number of "peace" hospitals. On one occasion, I was informed in a Chinese roundabout way that I was persona non grata with the Communists. On top of this, the Quakers, in particular, made me the object of their "prophetic" witness on behalf of the Communist side: I learned what it is to be on the receiving end of prophecy. Their prophetic protests seemed to be informed more by political preferences than by the facts of the case. Admittedly, my reaction may have been typically administrative, since I was not accustomed to public pressures. So I began to feel isolated and somewhat beleaguered.

As a young man in charge of a sensitive though relatively small operation, I felt the pain of public criticism. I learned in a small way at least what it means to act and to take the consequences. From my perspective, the role of prophet seemed all too easy. The moral advantage was always with the prophet, who seemed to protest with impunity, with an assumed righteousness born of traditional biblical presumption. By contrast, the administrator is identified with the establishment, which is routinely criticized or condemned for not having the capacity or the will to embody the ideal. I found myself resenting some of the criticism I received, especially when it appeared to be political bias clothed in religious piety.

As well, there were times when my staff and I were required to accept military escort. That bothered me, but I had to go along with it. Also it was necessary to call upon the military to protect supplies in transport. Police protection is accepted by most Christians as a matter of course, but to deliberately ask for military protection with a relatively high probability of violence was another problem that had to be faced. What if some Chinese recruits were to die because of our particular mission and status?

I could describe at greater length and poignancy the circumstances with which we were forced to come to terms with politics in a context of civil war. Possibly I was overly sensitive; certainly I was no seasoned public servant. But consider the following: (1) I headed an organization that made discriminate judgments favoring some people and organizations over others. In light of Jesus' refusal to make such judgments as a matter of principle, ("Man, who made me a divider over you?"–Luke 12:14; cf. Schleitheim Confession), should his followers not likewise refuse to make such judgments? (2) I brought punitive powers to bear against dishonest employees. "Evil doers" were not forgiven as a matter of course. In more than one case the Committee exposed specific corrupt practices and exacted penalties. (3) Though we tried to be just, undoubtedly we failed to be perfectly just. We may have deserved a measure of the "prophetic" complaints made against our organization. (4) I may have been influenced too much by political pressures at times, even though criticism appeared to be largely due to political bias rather than informed judgments.

(5) Amid the near anarchy of civil war, there were times when the lines between propriety and impropriety, truth and untruth, were hard to determine. But I never sanctioned exchanges on the black market or the falsification of documents, although U.S. Ambassador Leighton Stuart, at one time the highly respected New Testament scholar at Yen Jing University, suggested that the gap between official exchange rates and economic reality was so great that fairness to U.S. donors called for use of the black market. He seemed to anticipate Bonhoeffer's ethic of truth. (6) There may have been times when I failed to demonstrate genuine humility, though my colleagues urged me to be more assertive. (7) It was not clear how to give expression to one's identity as a Christian in a secular political context. Should I have been more deliberately and overtly Christian? I thought that faith must be expressed primarily through such ordinary virtues as honesty, hard work, cheerfulness, and fairness rather than verbal expression. Certainly one had no right to force Christian ideas on non-Christians. At best, one may expect "civil righteousness" in the public sphere–a rare commodity at times.

Nevertheless, my experience as Director of a UN Commission for one year brought me great joy and a sense of achievement. Its work saved some from death and made more bearable the lives of many. For example, to have been able to transfer (albeit on paper, so far as I was directly involved) complete surplus army and navy hospitals to the Chinese, despite the "politics" and the clash of partisan wills at the negotiation table, gave me a great sense of satisfaction.

But as a nonresistant, uncompromising perfectionist with no ethic of assertive power congruent with the clash of political interest and commercial competition, and with no provision for compromise and ambiguity, I was confused. To be sure, I had done nothing illegal, immoral, mean, indecent, dishonest, disorderly or selfish in the common, ordinary sense of such terms. My conduct was civil and conventional. I did only what was considered proper, indeed essential to orderly and just distribution of goods in a volatile historical situation.

Yet it was evident to my unsophisticated and uninformed mind that the world of politics, commerce, institutions, laws, national egos, and collective powers of all sorts–even denominational missions and "private agencies"–did not operate on the basis of *agape* alone. When pressed, all of them were prepared to defend their interests. All participated in the give-and-take of power structures, not just because it could not be otherwise, given the overall political and economic order, but because their very corporate structures predisposed them to adopt defensive postures and aggressive policies. Admittedly, both private and public organizations professed to be just, legal, considerate, reasonable, imaginative, generous, kind, and in some sense loving. But none did and presumably could "turn the other cheek" as a matter of policy, be defrauded rather than defend its interests at law, give upon demand apart from considerations of merit and conflicting obligations, or operate out of poverty and live by faith without prudential considerations. None of the players in the arena of collective life that I encountered took "no thought for the morrow." To do so would have led to chaos and irresponsibility, so said my Jewish lawyer friend and Chinese denominational leaders.

In my most probing hours of reflection while waiting for trains or planes with only a Bible at hand, I searched the Scripture for occasions when Jesus may have responded to issues such as I faced. I was intrigued by the parable of the Good Samaritan, a perfect illustration of love, reflecting Jesus' empathy for human beings, including minorities like Samaritan women. I assumed that Jesus loved especially poor people, cripples, people of other nationalities, and children. I knew that he never resisted his enemies by force though perhaps he did use elusive tactics in defense of his mission.

But I observed that in many ways his life was not representative of ordinary life. For one thing, Jesus never married and was not responsible for a spouse and children. As a bachelor and as an itinerant preacher and prophet, he did not have to worry about feeding a family, their security, giving them an education, and burying them if they died. Would Jesus have said, "Let the dead bury the dead," if his own child had died?

And Jesus did not run anything. He declared his independence from the religious establishment. He was not responsible for the founding and maintenance of a corporate organization–not even an organized fellowship. He defied authority; he did not report to a board or to a constituency; he disavowed most normal cultural ties. He was responsible only to God, whom he called his Father. Further, he paid no taxes so far as we know, and was not compelled to decide concretely what belongs to Caesar and what belongs to God. He was not drafted for war. When it comes to political authorities, he dealt with Jewish leaders and Roman Emperors who were not good though not as bad as Hitler. As a freelance, he was beholden to no one. He lived to be only thirty-three or so. What if he had lived to be seventy years of age and without family support? Would he have counseled his followers to "take no thought for the morrow?" If he had been a member of a community organized by some other person or authority, would he have "fit in"? If the poor are blessed, how poor and yet blessed? Surely the hundreds of starving Chinese whom I saw digging for winter roots on the hillsides of Tsing-tao were not blessed. He taught his disciples not to lord it over others as the Gentiles do.

How far do we carry Jesus' strictures against power and hierarchical orders? Will Jesus allow no vertical power structures at all? If not, how will anything of an organized nature get done? And if our real brothers and sisters are fellow believers and not natural kin, how can one meet the emotional and material needs of one's family? What about the bonding process between parent and child? Can one go the second mile while in the employ of others? Can one give away another's goods simply for having been asked? What about institutional life? Can institutions be operated within the parameters of a personal ethic? And what about discipleship in relation to kingship?

In this connection we may ask, What is the meaning of Jesus' triumphal entry into Jerusalem? Was it simply a symbol of uncoerced peace that would follow from Jesus' eschatological reign, when the world order would be metaphysically changed so that even the "lamb shall lie down with the lion"? Or is it to be interpreted as a nonviolent aborted coup? If so, would it be impious to speculate about how Jesus would have exercised kingship in a world like this, were he to have been accepted as King of Israel, the Messiah? What shape would his policies have taken? How would he have gotten along with the Romans? How would he have raised revenues? Would his court system have rendered punitive judgments, or would all sinners have been automatically forgiven or left untried, since no judges could have been found who were "without sin"? Would private ownership of property have been retained at least until the Jubilee Year? Would there have been police? How would the poor have been vindicated? And would the proud have been forgiven or would they have been "scattered in the imagination of their heart" (Luke 1:51)?

Maybe it seems frivolous to ask such questions, but not for disciples of Christ who seek to follow after him in a world whose structures have not yet been transformed into the Kingdom of God. It seemed to me that responsible participation in corporate structures and radical discipleship were in conflict. So far as personal ethics were concerned, problems appeared to be rooted mostly in the will: one could more or less "imitate" the life of Jesus as an unattached individual if one had the faith to do so. (Harriet and I lived very simply in Shanghai on an MCC allowance of $10 per person per month plus keep. We returned home with three little children, no furniture, no car, and no job, only a severance allowance from Church World Service.)

Where shall we look in Scripture for a model of public management where love is the essence? My consciousness of the tension between discipleship and public responsibility led us to decline an offer for work within the United Nations with good money and some prestige. To this day, we have no regrets. But I brought home the problem which I have pondered ever since. It can be stated in many ways: What is the relevance of Jesus' life and teachings for corporate structures? Is the ethic of Jesus an historical possibility? If Jesus' ethic is a personal ethic in substance as well as form, how can it become the basis for a social ethic? Could the problem be metaphysical? Is the culprit not only sin but complexity as well–a variation of the philosophical problem of the one and the many? The concept of the Kingdom of God is certainly a social, indeed a political, concept. Accordingly, Jesus was critical of the Jewish establishment for its not being a Kingdom of Heaven. But he gave us no blueprint of the Kingdom, no instruction of a procedural nature about how to transform historical structures into heavenly structures. Possibly it is good that he did not write a manifesto, lest his followers become ideological fanatics.

My reflections took place in loneliness while separated from my family for nearly three years, and with no one of a theological or philosophical inclination with whom I could discuss existential problems. My moods fluctuated from satisfaction at meaningful work done well and positive self-discovery to disappointment for not being able to give unambiguous social shape to the ethics of Jesus. In this respect I shared the experience of Luther, whose primary source of pain was his failure to embody the "law of God" in the socal situation.

The omnipresent sufferings of the Chinese people sometimes got through to me as well. I saw starving people die; I witnessed blood in the mud and snow from bare-footed coolies. I witnessed air accidents and hospitals filled with wounded soldiers, and I ran personal risks while flying under conditions that would not be countenanced today. It is amazing how "theologically minded" I became before and after flying as co-pilot of "St. Paul," a DC-3 in service of the Lutheran mission.

More was happening than I could place in proper perspective. Somehow I was beginning to develop a tragic view of reality as I became aware of the depth and persistence of systemic evil, the frailty of human flesh, and the ravages of nature. I was impressed with what supports and what destroys life. Food became almost sacramental. Distinctions between rudimentary essentials such as shelter and a bowl of noodles, and such amenities as higher education, art, and banquets became exaggerated. I pondered why some lived and others died, why children had to suffer and why disease devoured entire villages. One could explain evil resulting from war and the selfishness of army generals who hoarded grain, and from dislocations due to hardness of heart. But what about the randomness of famine and death? Goodness and evil seemed wrapped together as in a ball of string, the strands inseparable. Life ran together those days into a stream of indivisible reality except at its extremes. I struggled with an ontological view of sin which would account for sin as originating more in nature than in human guile. Ethics and ontology, history and nature, the private and public sectors, even church and society, while conceptually distinguishable, unexpectedly appeared to be interpenetrating and interdependent. Evidence of social solidarity challenged my inherited dualistic interpretations of society.

It seemed like half of my life was crowded into those four years in China. Shortly before Harriet and I were evacuated from Shanghai by the U.S. Navy as Communist forces approached the city, UNRRA invited me to continue under its director, Harlan Cleveland, U.S. President Grover Cleveland's grandson. To accept this honor would have meant a career in the secular world rather than a vocation in the church, so I declined it.

III

When we returned to the U.S. in 1949, I brought back two strong and evidently contradictory convictions. One was that *agape* is the ultimate reality by which all human relations must be judged–*agape* as free-flowing, unlimited, forgiving, nonresistant, unmerited, unconditional, grace transcending all values as God transcends all else including his own creation. "God is love." I knew of no religious teacher or philosopher who taught unreciprocating love as did Jesus Christ, and none other embodied *agape* love as he did in his life and especially his death on the cross.

The second conviction was that to work on behalf of the poor in the world, even in the political world, seemed legitimate. I had been called to do the best I could in the field of competing powers and conflicting interests. People had to be fed, clothed, and healed. An avenue of significant effectiveness was to use corporate, indeed political power for the sake of other people. Responsibility could mean living and working accountably within the framework of the political world.

Harriet and I were now introduced to a theological and ethical context that was amazingly fixed, entrenched, institutionalized, confident, and triumphant. Maybe that is not how Harold Bender, Guy Hershberger, and the Concern Group felt about normative Anabaptism.[3] Possibly the leaders of the church felt that the Mennonite tradition was so insecure that only clear mandates and uncompromising ideological formulations could preserve the denomination. It was a heady time. Theology and ethics were defined by Bender's "The Anabaptist Vision" and Hershberger's *War, Peace and Nonresistance*. Members of the Concern Group came home from Europe during the 1950s, having had the enviable opportunity to study under such great theologians and philosophers as Barth, Brunner, Bultmann, Jaspers, Cullmann, and lesser figures. Against the backdrop of reformulations of classical Protestantism and existential philosophy, they were intent upon setting forth the Mennonite faith in terms of radical "dissent." This dissent went beyond the issue of war: it was presented as an alternative view of Christianity. Obviously, it was strongly influenced by historical studies of Anabaptism, and by Troeltsch's *The Social Teachings of the Christian Churches*, with its distinction between the "church type" and the "sect type." The Concern Group spoke without embarrassment about being consistently "sectarian," with social "irresponsibility" as a key concept. Ironically, with this ideology they turned their youthful ideas of radical discipleship and communitarian doctrines against Bender and other church

3 For a brief historical and analytical account of the Concern Movement, see J. L. Burkholder, "Concern Pamphlets Movement," *Mennonite Encyclopedia*, V, 177-80.

leaders held responsible for the compromises of the Mennonite church. Criticism was not directed at the "Vision" itself but at the failure of the Mennonite church to embody it.

I could not help but respect, indeed envy, my younger peers who had had the advantage of European graduate education at a most exciting period of theological development. While they read original manuscripts of famous authors, I read shipping manifests and flew airplanes and argued with insurance underwriters. But I simply could not identify wholeheartedly with sectarian theology. It seemed to me to be too narrow, too simplistic, too arbitrary and unrealistic when it comes to life in this world, of which I had had quite a dose. The "Anabaptist Vision" made a lot of sense at the "communion table," where discipleship and *agape* love alone are the essence. But what about the "negotiation table," where egos, especially corporate egos, function as competing powers? Even a trip to the neighborhood store would indicate that exchange of goods for money in a capitalistic economy is not an expression of love alone. Where in the capitalistic structure would you hear words comparable to these of Isaiah: "Come all you who are thirsty, come to the waters, and you who have no money, come buy and eat! Come . . . without money and without cost" (Isaiah 55:1)? True, the Mennonites had long preached nonconformity, and to a certain extent separated themselves from the world, but not so skillfully as to extricate themselves from its competitive struggles. My experience had led me to believe that even the most withdrawn and consistent sectarians who love each other nevertheless presumably deal with each other justly. But justice was not even acknowledged as a Christian category in those days. Justice is a Greek concept, it was claimed, and as such it belongs to the "polis," not to the church. Christians have no need for such a concept. They should always aim at love, never insisting upon justice for themselves or others, said Guy Hershberger. Between Jerusalem and Athens there can be little more than suspicion.

But quite apart from problems of consistency in the application of sectarian idealism, I appreciated the beauty, the logical consistency, the biblical basis, and the moral appeal of a form of Christianity that would be not only christological but radical in its application of the life of Jesus as some sort of "imitation." Who can argue with the Apostles, St. Francis, martyred Anabaptists, saintly mothers, and a hero such as Bonhoeffer? Indeed, it was Bonhoeffer's *Cost of Discipleship* that kept me from being turned off by sectarian pride and triumphalism. To me, Bonhoeffer's theology of discipleship was terribly attractive, especially because he seemed to choose Christian radicality while knowing the classical tradition from the inside. So I nearly memorized the *Cost of Discipleship*, and when I was asked to teach at Goshen College, I taught a course on discipleship, a subject long since dropped from the curricula of Mennonite colleges and seminaries. A paragraph from Bonhoeffer struck me with the authority of a text from the Bible itself: "The disciple simply burns his boats and goes ahead . . . . The old life is left behind, and completely surrendered. The disciple is dragged out of his relative security into a life of absolute insecurity, from a life that is observable and calculable into a life where everything is unobservable and fortuitous, out of the realm of finite, and into the realm of infinite possibilities . . . . Discipleship means Jesus Christ, and Him alone. It cannot consist of anything more than that."[4]

I knew, having studied Bonhoeffer, that whatever form the Christian life may take in relation to culture, it must contain elements of risk, adventure, indeterminacy, sacrifice, obedience, and openness to the Spirit. It must be lived with, and under the disciplinary love of, the church. My reflection upon radical discipleship was also accompanied by concern for the renewal of the church. Creative possibilities of the house church, small groups, and lay participation made a considerable impression on me.

But my troubles with the Anabaptist Vision made me less than a true believer. As a young radical, I was nevertheless a realist–yet not like most realists, whose struggles have to do mainly, if not entirely, with the human propensity for sin. For I was also concerned about dilemmas grounded in the condition of finite existence in relation to structured power. To be sure, Mennonites addressed problems of power as they pertained to the "world" outside the Mennonite community. It was obvious to Hershberger that economic power as embodied in organized labor and litigation violated the ethic of nonresistance. But he failed to understand the power implicit in property and enterprise, and especially institutional life. His criticism of Gandhi was logical from a Mennonite perspective, but his complete failure to understand the universal dynamics of power, within which even Goshen College participated, left me stunned. My experience in China had convinced me that social intervention is never totally disinterested and, as stated earlier, helps some and sometimes even hurts others. There is no such thing as unambiguous social power. That Hershberger and other contemporary "Anabaptists" could not see that, and would not even discuss the inevitable problematics of Mennonite power, amazed me. What was especially disturbing was the fact that questions were treated as signs of disloyalty to the tradition. Even worse, problems with Anabaptism were treated, it seemed, as a lack of faithfulness to Christ. In the early 1950s, Goshen seemed closed to criticism; The Anabaptist Vision was final and definitive. I found that I could not question the establishment and get away with it. To question was self-recriminating. Consequently, "truth" and "community" seemed in conflict.

I pondered the propriety of stating openly my questions about the finality of Anabaptism and about the inerrancy of Scripture. Concern for the truth as I saw it impelled me to reveal my dissent. But I was also aware that the church was,

4 Dietrich Bonhoeffer, *The Cost of Discipleship* (London: MacMillan, 1959), 51.

after all, the body of Christ, within which unity was an essential value. Unfortunately, at that time I was critical of what were considered core beliefs, not nonessentials. To challenge core beliefs is always threatening; after all, truth as well as falsehood can be fragmenting. The counsel of the Apostle Paul to the so-called "knowledgeable" of the church at Corinth about the propriety of eating food for idols applied to this upstart college teacher: "Only take care lest this liberty becomes a stumbling block to the weak" (1 Cor. 8:9). Without debating who was weak and who was strong, I muted my criticisms, having somewhat satisfied my integrity by refusing to sign the doctrinal statement as it referred to the inerrancy of Scripture.

My feeling then as now is that dissent must be finessed, lest it do more harm than good. Dissenters do well not to provoke the extreme reaction of those responsible for the maintenance of the tradition. Further, not all matters of dissent are "Copernican" in significance and scope. Indeed, one of my criticisms of certain sixteenth-century Anabaptist groups is that in their zeal for the truth as they saw it, they were not sufficiently cognizant of the unity of Christian civilization. It is ironic that concern for unity, which unfortunately led the major reformers to persecute dissent, also prompted the leaders of the Mennonite Church in the twentieth century to disallow ideas considered threatening.

Of course, the 1950s must be placed in perspective. It was a time when the Mennonite church was trying to find a self-respecting place in Christendom. It was still in the early stages of historical and theological identity formation. Anabaptism was being interpreted as a theological alternative for the scholarly world and as a viable form of Christianity even in modern times. All of us owe a great deal to the leaders of that time. But writers of manifestos and creators, as well as recreators, of religious movements are seldom given to the downside. Manifestos are not confessionals, and they always overstate the case. Further, ideological formation is by its very nature inhospitable to alternative views. A premium is placed upon differences, not upon common ground. To define is to differentiate, and to differentiate is to separate, so it seemed.

If the Mennonite theological leadership appeared assured and dogmatic, theirs was not an isolated case. That was how even ecumenical theologians conducted their business at the time. Karl Barth could entitle his polemic against natural theology with the arresting but less than generous, *Nein, Herr Brunner*, and the preponderant prepositional use of "over-against" (*gegenüber*) signaled the propensity of virtually all traditions to redefine Reformation faith within the presuppositions of a still confident but highly differentiated and polemical Christendom. Further, the tendency to reduce history and theology to "ideology" antedated those changes in human consciousness, leading subsequently to the "end of ideology."

While affirming points of emphasis in Anabaptism, I could not accept it uncritically in its ideological form. I felt there was more to Christianity than could be contained within the idea of the isolated Mennonite community and a theology of dissent. I was not ready at that time to challenge central insights of the sectarian tradition outright, but I was prepared to say that Christianity should not be so narrowly conceived if it were to express the "fulness" of Christ, let alone the incontrovertible fact of solidarity of even the "nonconformed" with society at large. I simply could not look foward to the necessity of bootlegging such cultural realities as art, philosophy, business, and politics into the Christian community.

I had not heard of "ontology" or "reality testing" in those days, but simple honesty seemed to demand a more critical and less polemical approach to church history, to other denominations, and to secular democratic and humane institutions than I found among certain Mennonite leaders and young reformers. I pondered the role of pride as an essential ingredient of communal cohesion, and the propensity of a small sectarian denomination to beat up on Christendom as if its roots were elsewhere. As well, I questioned polemical ethics for its concentration upon the failures of others rather than upon honest acknowledgement of one's own participation in the relativities of historical existence. But I would be less than honest if I were to present myself as a confident theologian; I was simply trying to find myself as a young teacher, whose achievements to date had to do more with shipping documents and office memos than with the Bible and church history.

The ethical question that dominated my thinking was formulated in connection with teaching discipleship. Granted that we are all commanded to love God and the neighbor as oneself, what does this commandment mean concretely? If we may assume that love is the ground, the motive, the primary principle of judgment for all that we do, and as such is the starting point for any system of ethics, how do we move from the love of God in Christ to its concrete application? What form do Jesus and his teachings imply for life in our time?

As a Mennonite who belonged to the Schleitheim tradition and as a disciple of the early Bonhoeffer, I believed that the life and teachings of Christ must be taken not only seriously but literally within reasonable bounds of critical interpretation. That is, we must take Jesus' sayings seriously as presented in the Gospels without modernizing or spiritualizing them. Of course, we must not literalize to the point of legalistic absurdity as if, for example, we were to insist upon preaching to the Eskimos barefooted because of Jesus' instructions to the seventy (Luke 10:4). Discipleship begins with faith, commitment, and loyalty to Christ as conditions of the mind and heart. But it is concerned with more than motive: It also concerns the shape, the form, of the external act as well. If discipleship were limited to loyalty, no basis for distinctions between those who are loyal and those who are disloyal would be available. After all, who was most committed to Christ: Luther, Zwingli, John Knox, or Menno? Only God knows. And who cares? Discipleship stands for both the inner life and the outer life. But what is distinctive about genuine discipleship is primarily a matter of styles of life. In general, to follow after Jesus in our time is to do what Jesus did, or what Jesus would do today in similar situations on the basis of what he did do.

To me, discipleship continued to mean imitation–loosely constructed, of course–as well as a process of abstracting from Jesus' teachings the principles which should be applied in appropriate situations. This meant to be nonresistant or at least nonviolent, to be sacrificial, to embrace "functional" poverty, to place the Kingdom of God even above family and obligations imposed by nature, to have vocational mobility, to take up cross bearing, to prefer the welfare of others to one's own, to refuse to use power over others for personal benefit, to love the enemy, and in general, to make one's life and property available to others, especially to brothers and sisters in the faith. Harriet and I were intent upon maintaining patterns of radical discipleship which, in some respects, were not really voluntary as members of the Goshen College community! When we returned from China we had no money and no power, no reputation and no professional mobility, indeed, no profession.

The context for radical discipleship seemed to be limited to church vocations in those days. Didn't Jesus call his disciples away from secular vocations to Kingdom work? One implication of discipleship was the depreciation of earthly affairs. From the standpoint of eschatological claims, anything that had to do with making life possible and sustainable, let alone fulfilling, was subordinated to Kingdom concerns. Recall the Mary and Martha story, which epitomizes the New Testament attitude toward work as a necessary but relatively meaningless endeavor. Work was justified by the Apostle Paul as a means for sharing with other Christians but not for its intrinsic value or for its support of the social order. Those in positions of economic and political power became the object of Jesus' harshest criticism. To enter the Kingdom, rich and powerful people had to repent of their wealth and their power. Anything established comes under the criticism of the "trans-valuation of values," as Nietzsche reminds us. Worldly values are put down, not because they are temporal or material but because they fall short of the eschatological vision of a totally transformed order. In the Gospels as well as in the whole New Testament corpus, the world is perceived as passing away and to be replaced. In the meantime, life is a holding action. Hence, what emerged in the first century was at best the early stages of a communal ethic but certainly no social ethic. In Paul's first letter to the church at Corinth he prefaces practical instructions with eschatological expectations "as you eagerly wait for our Lord Jesus Christ to be revealed" (1 Cor. 1:7).

I seldom doubted the validity and the authority of the eschatological vision. The vocational call to be an obedient disciple of Christ I could not resist. But I was fascinated with the world and its structures at the same time. By structures I mean the organizational configurations by which people live together and accomplish purposes essential to personal and corporate life–family, education, economics, politics, law, medicine, aesthetics, and organized religions, all of which make up the world. Of course, I was concerned that worldly structures are fallen at least to such an extent as to accommodate selfish purposes, though within limits imposed by truth and justice. Worldly structures are ambiguous at best. That most Christians must live in such a world is obvious; only a few live as celibates within monasteries.

Therefore, I was compelled to ask how Christians can live in the world as contributors to creative processes and as responsible agents for God, and not by accident or by necessity but as a Christian calling, I found no New Testament warrant for responsible, purposeful involvement in the world of economics and politics beyond keeping body and soul together while serving the church. Why invest one's energies in an order that is passing away? But as a young man, I felt that the world–that which lies beyond the ecclesia–is where most people are. They are to be loved, and one way (certainly not the only way) is to work in and through and with "unredeemed," i.e., ambiguous, public orders. I began to feel on the basis of my work in China that even politics is not only a legitimate but needful Christian vocation.

In the Bender/Hershberger/Concern period, the idea of politics as a vocation was simply unthinkable and therefore inadmissible. "Inadmissible" was the word frequently used to designate the inappropriateness of my questions. Responsibility could not be reconciled with the powerlessness of the "way of the cross," and the relative insignificance of the world, given the claim that God's redemptive purposes are accomplished in the church and only in a secondary way, if at all, through the political realm. My inclinations were to refuse such simple either-or solutions to the problem as those of Bender, Hershberger and Concern in the 1950s, when Schleitheim, the undisputed source of Mennonite ethics, pointed to a clean, consistent, and undivided ethic of withdrawal.

Princeton, 1951

I thus entered graduate studies at Princeton Theological Seminary in 1951 with a problem of many layers and ramifications. Unfortunately, I felt alone and alienated from my tradition. I had been placed on probation at Goshen in effect, if not officially, since I could not sign the Garden City confession (1921) as it pertained to the inerrancy of Scripture. Imagine being required to teach the Genesis account of beginnings as history and the ethics of the conquest of Canaan from a fundamentalist view of inspiration, which Goshen had picked up from the Old Princeton or from less scholarly places.

What I discovered at Princeton was that the issues with which I struggled in my innocence were not idiosyncratic. They were not just mine, they were classical issues of Christendom. What do we do with a perfectionistic ethic born amid the particularity of Israel, taught and modeled by a single person in an eschatological setting where it was presumed that the end of history is imminent? What do we make of the fact that history did not end as expected and promised? If we begin with the presupposition, as Christians must, that Jesus is normative for all generations and all conditions, how does Jesus "function" as the norm long after eschatological expectations dim, time moves on, cultures evolve and interact, nations rise and fall–and as the church, instead of living in expectation of an imminent end, must decide what to do with itself and with the world after Christians are no longer simply "pilgrims and strangers" (eschatology having become for most Christians not the end of history but the certainty of their own mortality amid the transience of "all things" in an evolving universe of billions of years)?

In my study of the historical and dogmatic literature, I was amazed by the proliferation of views on any and all subjects that emerged in Christian thought throughout the centuries. Many views were contradictory, yet each was "justified" by appeals to Scripture. As a Mennonite, I had become accustomed to differences between Old Testament theology and New Testament theology. But at Princeton, it became evident to me that even the New Testament is ambivalent on many foundational matters. Different views on Christology, the relation of mercy to judgment, the immortality of the soul, the use of the Old Testament, law and grace, attitudes toward the Jewish nation–these and many more issues remained unresolved. And with respect to to Christian history, two dimensions continuously came to mind–the particularity of Jesus and the claims of universality.

My impression was that Mennonite strength lay in its commitment to the particular in a rather severe either-or, all or nothing, adherence to Jesus only, especially Matthean, discipleship. Accordingly, Mennonites insisted upon a strong but short tether–strong communitarian ties but short in regard to responsible participation in the larger culture and what some would call the "orders of creation." Mennonites planted both feet closely, stubbornly, and uncompromisingly on Christian communal ground, intent upon bringing people of the world into the "perfection of Christ," one by one. Remember Harold Bender in "The Anabaptist Vision" disavows the "Christianization" of social structures. After comparing the Anabaptist vision with major Reformation traditions, he says, "Since for him (the Anabaptist) no compromise dare be made with evil, the Christian may in no circumstance participate in any conduct in the existing social order which is contrary to the spirit and teaching of Christ and the apostolic practice. He must consequently withdraw from the worldly system and create a Christian social order within the fellowship of the church brotherhood. Extension of this Christian order by the conversion of individuals and their transfer out of the world into the church is the only way by which progress can be made in Christianizing the social order."

But upon reading Troeltsch and others, I became aware of the claims of universality which Troeltsch insisted were not only implied by classical philosophical speculation but were implicit within the Gospel as well. He insisted that universal implications were introduced into the Christian tradition by the Apostle Paul, especially since he accepted, by missionary necessity if not by choice, the family. Marriage may appear to be innocent in itself, but by virtue of its dependence upon civilization for commerce, education, security, law, and art, the Christian community gradually and inextricably entered into a relation of reciprocal give-and-take with the world. Civilization is more than the family writ large, but given time, the family requires civilization for its sustenance. It became inevitable that Christianity, a Jewish religion, would come to terms for its own self-understanding, let alone for polemical purposes, with universal reason as represented by Jewish speculation and Gentile philosophy. Justin Martyr, the Christian apologist (ca. 150 AD), represented a stage in the development of the Christian community when its central concepts were examined in light of general knowledge, a development foreshadowed in the logos Christologies of Ephesians and Colossians. If we are to understand the transition from Christianity to Christendom, we would do well to see this not only or primarily in connection with the conversion of Constantine and the political union of the church and the state, but with the tendency of the church to see itself in light of universal experience. Thus I wondered whether Anabaptist radicalism should be interpreted as pure genius or as arrested development. Is sectarian radicality to be lauded for its ability to go to the root of things as it claims, or is it an embryo clutching at the womb, unwilling to be born?

The history of Christian ethics seemed to me to be the adjustment of an eschatological religion to the essential elements of life in this world. If the Corpus Christianum had not taken the form it did, it would have taken some other form. It is inevitable that Christianity would somehow, some time, respond to the family, politics, education, economics, science, philosophy, art, music, history, and nature. The tether would have to be lengthened, not necessarily by its encounter with external systems of thought but by its own inner dynamics. The Roman Catholic tradition lengthened its tether to address all issues pertaining to life in this world as a responsible participant in human affairs. Thus I felt drawn in both directions–the rigor of radical discipleship within the sectarian community and the "fulness" of Catholicity in which, quite apart from Constantinianism, an attempt is made to bring Christ to bear upon "all things" essential to human existence.

Current during the post-war period in Europe and America, and especially within ecumenical discussions, was the concept of "social responsibility." The concept of responsibility as a way to express duty goes back to British moral philosopher F.H. Bradley and his essay, "The Vulgar Notion of Responsibility . . ." (1876). It was implicit within the ethics of classical Christianity (Catholic and Protestant), but it emerged after World War II explicitly as a general term by which to describe how Christians and churches should be related to the social order. Literature on the "responsible society" followed the meeting of the World Council of Churches in Amsterdam (1948).

Behind the concern for social responsibility lay the failure of the churches to resist Hitler. After World War II, all major religious traditions vigorously devoted their energies to theological reconstruction, including ethics in the grand style of system formation. The concept of responsibility was of course ambiguous. But like truth, it was convincing enough to be accepted without clarity, especially since its opposite was unthinkable.

By contrast, for Mennonites "social irresponsibility" was not unthinkable. Indeed, "social irresponsibility" was declared in *Concern* No.1 (1954) by John Howard Yoder as an implication of the Mennonite view of the church. Not to be responsible for the moral decision-making of society at large is an implication of discipleship and must be made a presupposition of Mennonite ecclesiology. Not to be responsible is not a matter of neglect rooted in a lack of social awareness but is rather a logical implication of the sectarian ethic. "We should not be ashamed of our 'irresponsibility'," Yoder declared.

I could not disagree with the logic of sectarian ecclesiology, but I could not be happy with it. I recall a casual conversation with Paul Ramsey when I expressed some equivocation about responsibility for the world. I said, "I am not sure that I can accept social responsibility" Ramsey replied, "But you are responsible." I was shocked by the presumed self-evidence ofhis statement. I had to agree that was how I felt, but I didn't know how to respond to its axiomatic character. I was not clear how to understand responsibility concretely, and as a Mennonite pacifist I was not sure how I could accept responsiblity as a controling presupposition of social ethics.

I decided that social responsibility in relation to Mennonite ethics should be the focus of my doctoral thesis. This should have been easy, since I knew more about the Mennonites than did my examiners! But I soon found that to know what I was talking about, I would have to go through an avalanche of literature following Amsterdam (1948), and I must understand what led mainline theologians, ancient and modern, to assume that the concept of responsibility should be taken for granted. Since Professor Paul Lehman, who had done no more than approve my topic, left Princeton for Harvard in the middle 1950s, I was left without an advisor. I worked under no one. Hence, I had no idea whether my ruminations would make sense. Only upon the final examination did Princeton professors even know what I was writing about. As it turned out, my thesis got a summa cum laude.

Although the body of the thesis was about Mennonites, I felt I needed a grasp of Barth, Brunner, Ramsey, Tillich, Bultmann, Bonhoeffer, Paul Lehmann, the Niebuhrs, et al. Also, I had to know more about the Corpus Christianum than that it was bad! The thesis was quite comprehensive and I feared that it might be disqualified for its sweeping generalizations and its subjectivity. Fortunately, it appeared convincingly right to the examiners, but obviously unacceptable to my Mennonite brethren.[5]

In that thesis I tried to place Mennonite thought and life in a good light. I set forth such ideas as discipleship and Anabaptism analytically as best I could. I described what Anabaptism was up to, depending largely upon the accepted Goshen interpretation. I tried to set forth in broad outline Mennonite communal history and church-controlled efforts such as voluntary service, MCC, missions, etc.

But in the final chapter, entitled "The Challenge of the Responsible Society," and in the Conclusion, I proposed that as Mennonites become increasingly urbanized and participate in business and professional life, and as their educational levels rise and their imaginations are stimulated, they are bound to develop a more comprehensive view of the world and will come to recognize increasingly their involvement in, dependence upon, and responsibility for it. Hence, the question is whether these developments can occur within the limits imposed by the Anabaptist Vision as defined by Bender, or whether a more realistic and inclusive Mennonite vision be constructed which is more representative of social reality and modern thought.

I contended that the Mennonites, while embodying love and nonresistance, had failed to come to terms with some essential components of a social ethic. To be sure, Mennonite theologians and historians had interpreted the Gospel in such a way as to encourage brotherhood in community and to be good neighbors, honest business men and women, and to engage in effective programs of church-sponsored relief and rehabilitation. Mennonite post-World War II relief efforts had become widespread, earning considerable respect in many parts of the world.

But their analysis of the social situation so far as ethics is concerned was too simple. The ethics of nonresistance served to answer the simple questions of what should I as an individual do (or what should we as a denomination do) if someone does us harm, and what shall we do for an immediate neighbor in need? But the social situation in which public welfare workers, mayors, bankers, hospital managers, college presidents, and political leaders find themselves is not simple but multilateral. Diagonal claims are brought to bear from many directions, and conflicts of interest bring dilemma after dilemma. In a complex situation it is not enough to be nonresistant. One must decide what to do in light of many social, economic, and political forces, some of which lie beyond one's control. The time is past when one can avoid the claims and counter-claims of a dynamic society not only in flux but even in contest with itself.

Traditional Mennonite ethics had failed to come to terms with this social

5 Published some thirty years later as *The Problem of Social Responsibility from the Perspective of the Mennonite Church* (Elkhart, Indiana: Institute of Mennonite Studies, 1989).

reality. Life in the world is not just one simple situation after another. It is thousands of interacting, intersecting, interested parties in relation to one another, resulting sometimes in high-minded cooperation and sometimes in outright opposition while being regulated by religious values, liberal sentiments, just laws, and balances of power. Hence, love in the social realm is preferential and thwarted by moral conflict.

It seemed evident to me that in order to change the world rather than to overcome the world in absentia, it will be necessary for Mennonites to introduce into the ethical calculus ideas hitherto neglected or deliberately rejected. These ideas would have to be defined and related to one another on theretical as well as practical levels–a monumental and troublesome task, since they represent realities which do not at first appear to be easily related to one another and especially with *agape* love. What this means is that Mennonites will no longer weather the storm by taking cover in convenient harbors of their own making but by steering the best possible courses on the high seas of history.

Some of the new ideas are, of course, as old as the second century after Christ and about them a vast literature has been written. Their definition, assessment, emphasis, ordering, and application in relation to *agape* love is what distinguishes one system from another within Christendom. Some of these ideas are: resistance (nonviolent and violent); ambiguity (metaphysical and moral); justice (distributive and punitive); power (personal, corporate, and political); compromise (positive and negative); and grace (enabling and forgiving).

My contention was that such concepts are unavoidable, since they represent what is. Obviously, "thereness" does not necessarily imply "rightness," but thereness, by which I mean reality ontologically perceived, implies dialectics. After all, the world is structured dialectically; reality is not of one piece. Polarities that may be ontologically verified do not necessarily relate to one another easily. For that very reason, Christendom has been "confused," to acknowledge Tillich's contention in *Love, Power and Justice.* If Christendom of nearly two thousand years is confused about how to get love, power, and justice together, Mennonites may understandably be in for a challenging time of ethical reformulation.

Little wonder that my thesis was offensive to Mennonite leadership. I had challenged the finality of Mennonite thinking at that time by insisting that great, historic ethical issues on the methodological level could no longer be avoided through sectarian denials.

I would insist, however, that traditional Mennonite thinking as set forth in its most consistent and radical formulations after World War II, especially by the Concern Group, must be taken seriously. Sectarian theology and ethics cannot be dismissed simply as youthful idealism and sociological naivete. As far as it goes, sectarianism is an authentic and consistent expression of the Gospel of Jesus Christ with roots in a literal and binding understanding of Jesus' teaching and its communal implications. It calls for clear differentiations between the church and the world, between communal discipline and accommodation. Say what you will, traditional Mennonite leaders were right when they saw in world systems much that is evil, such as greed, vanity, pride, injustice, and exploitation. They insisted without flinching that the world is lost and needs to be saved. And they were right when they saw in the conversion of individuals the primary strategy for the salvation of the world. Even H. Richard Niebuhr could write a monograph entitled *The Church Against the World* (1935), and in *Christ and Culture* (1951), he expressed the view that the position "Christ against culture" is "both logically and chronologically entitled to the first position; logically, because it appears to follow directly from the common Christian principle of the Lordship of Jesus Christ; chronologically, because it is widely held to be the typical attitude of the first Christians."[6]

If, therefore, Bender and his generation together with his disciples had not recovered the Anabaptist Vision, someone else would have had to formulate something like it. For what Troeltsch called sectarianism is as essential to Christianity as ontology is to realism. Both are there in their own way. Both must be taken dead seriously despite their one-sidedness when taken alone. Therefore, if one were to depart from sectarian radicalism to more accommodating intellectual systems and lifestyles, such departures may be done for one reason only, and that is to serve Christ by loving the neighbor with greater understanding and effectiveness.

In the 1950s I was forced to speculate about what kind of world we were living living in. On the basis of my experience in China and the post-World War II emphasis upon existentialism, I found it difficult to believe in the unity of reality. Every natural and historical phenomenon seemed to imply an opposite. Reality seemed to be polarized, so much so that I could not think without the employment of dialectics. Tension between evidently contradictory but equally true ideas became my habit of thought: everything seemed to be "over against" something else. Like everyone, I spoke about the created world as if it were an entity though, of course, without knowing its bounds. I spoke about the universe meaning "all that I was aware of" but without being sure what I was talking about. The oneness of the universe became almost as problematic as the oneness of God. Along with coherence for which there was evidence, I became aware of incoherence for which there also was evidence. Truth seemed to be a mixture of contrasting if not contradictory claims, and invariably I came to think increasingly in terms of paradox. I became suspicious of closed systems, and anything simple became suspect for its partial representation of the truth. I insisted upon both sides of an argument. The use of "and" and "but" became an unconscious stylistic pattern of my writing and speaking, signaling complexity and dialectics. I thought dialectically as I became aware of polarities, some

6 H. Richard Niebuhr, *Christ Against Culture* (New York, 1951), 45.

metaphysical, some historical, some theological, and some even scientific, insofar as I understood the natural world.

One problem which had impressed me in China was the paradox of freedom and responsibility, a problem as old as theology and philosophy. I had to ask whether Chinese refugees should be held accountable for truthfulness. My initial inclination as a good Mennonite was to insist upon moral freedom as an implication of accountability to God, if not human dignity. But I noticed that starving Chinese would almost invariably lie in accordance with the degree of their indigence, especially parents with children. So I wondered whether moral failure could be "caused" by hunger pains in the stomach and anxiety for the welfare of dependents. If starving refugees could not be counted on to tell the truth, maybe starvation itself, sometimes a condition of nature alone, could be blamed.

When upon returning from China I read Reinhold Niebuhr on the subject of sin, where he claims anxiety is the occasion for sin but not its cause, I felt that he failed to let his propensity for paradox have its sway. He over-simplified–a terrible thing to say about Niebuhr! I was ready to say on the basis of my limited experience that human beings are both morally free and determined, hardly a rational claim, but not without a kind of Kantian "practical" sense.

I was moved to pity the Chinese, and the longer I stayed in China the less prone I was to blame poor peasants and impressed soldiers. Increasingly I saw the human scene less as a divinely created plain of moral judgment but more as an abyss of tragic fate. People seemed to be caught by circumstances beyond their control. Freedom to determine one's destiny was the privilege of the well born and the rich, if of anyone, whereas the peasantry in Central China were condemned by birth to privation and suffering. Hence, ethics for me became not just what one does with one's freedom but how one comes to terms with the necessary conditions of nature as well. All this called for a theological reconstruction which takes into account a dialectical worldview of contrasts, paradoxes, metaphysical opposites, and dualities of various sorts. Since reality is dialectically structured, Christian theology does what it can to make sense out of the contrasting dimensions of reality.

I came out of China and away from Princeton with the feeling that reality as we experience it is ambiguous, and that the task of ethics is not simply to wrestle with the problem of sin and guilt but also with the problem of evil, these being compounded in light of the complexities of creation. We cannot change what is metaphysical, but we must take metaphysics seriously if we are to deal with our problems honestly and realistically.

IV

My doctoral thesis was rejected out of hand by Mennonites (old and young) in the 1950s, and it could not be published. Regretably, it was not even discussed openly; it was simply "inadmissible." "We cannot have this," said a dominant leader of the church. It struck too directly at certain Anabaptist presuppositions and core beliefs. I said by implication that the ethic of Jesus, especially as set forth by the Sermon on the Mount and the "hard sayings" which presupposed simple one-to-one situations, is not an historical social possibility, because the ethical situation is ambiguous, ambiguity being grounded in nature and compounded by history. Therefore, one must do the best possible, which unfortunately will necessitate compromise. Compromise is, of course, a complex idea, but it allowed what Anabaptism denied. While Mennonites were counseling "Try harder," I was saying, "Yes, try harder still," but in the context of the world where people are helped, albeit by proximate realizations of the ideal.

Justice

Specifically, justice was a problem. Hershberger assigned justice to the world of labor relations, civil strife, and politics. According to him, Christians must live by *agape* alone. He conceded that Christians must at least "do justice," by which he meant to act with nothing less ethical than justice. But one should not insist upon justice for oneself or for others. To the contrary, my contention was that social reality at its best involves dynamic interaction between *agape* and justice. Ideally they are inseparable. Justice is or at least can be a "mode" of love; it is love parceled out, divided, distributed. But since justice implies limits and is ordinarily both defined and defended by law and presupposes power and punishment in the breach, it cannot be equated with *agape*. Justice is love come to terms with multiplicity and institutional organization.

But justice is a complex concept. It always expresses an underlying spirit, and that spirit may not always be love. Sometimes justice, in this dog-eat-dog world, may be no more than an honorable truce between competing interests. It may even degenerate into a Maginot Line separating enemies. Justice is sometimes enmity bridled to manageable terms. A fence line may define the conditions by which neighborly care is justly ordered. But it may also function as a buffer between estranged neighbors. Therefore, the difference in spirit between amicable justice and legal justice must always be kept in mind. In the welter of corporate life, both in the economic and political sectors and even in the life of church institutions, justice is the most commonly assumed operational principle.

In *The Way of the Cross* (1958), Hershberger seemed say that the "cross" is a comprehensive rule, a total way of life. But I felt then as now that to make the cross the sole principle of continuous interaction is a contradiction and is in reality to deny the cross of its ultimate implications, namely total loss. The cross is by its nature an event but not a process which, when set forth theoretically, can be spoken of as a rule.

With regard to ambiguity, I contended that the world is a sea of good and evil, multiple demands, and three-way obligations (triage) that make "tragic necessity" inevitable. That is the way that nature and history cohere. This is not to deny untold opportunities to do good in this world–even to "transform" it here and there. Neighbors of all kinds cry out for help, and it is possible to make a difference if one is truly dedicated to what is good. Selfishness is the main problem. But the most selfless person runs into the problem of ambiguity when, for example, one adopts institutional budgets, disciplines evil doers, and manages other people's business. Ambiguity imposes limits. Hence, Christians experience genuine dilemmas, not just "seeming" dilemmas. (It was in 1981 at a General Conference meeting at Allentown, Pennsylvania, that Mennonite ethicists for the first time officially acknowledged that there is such a thing in this world as a "dilemma." Interestingly, in the same document it was claimed that dilemmas are "rare." Tell that to sensitive business men, mayors, social workers, medical researchers, college presidents, and statesmen.)

Historically, justice has not been accepted as a Christian category by Mennonites. Regarding power, no theoretical provision was made for its use in the Anabaptist-Mennonite lexicon. Everybody knows that power is used, but it was not acknowledged. Mennonites used power while exalting weakness. In so doing, they opened themselves to criticisms of naivete or hypocrisy or a combination thereof. Power is for real, and it is a problem even to those who acknowledge its theoretical inevitability. The main point of an ontological analysis of love, power, and justice à la Tillich is that all must be dealt with without cancelling each other out. They are facts of existence. Ambiguity is the term to describe conditions of the world that prevent their perfect correlation. Only in heaven, that state which transcends nature and history, is reality unambiguous. About that we can only speculate, since Heaven, like God, lies beyond experience.

Ambiguity

The concept of ambiguity is itself ambiguous, but no more so than other general terms that are broadly used, such as power, freedom, causation, nature, and history. An ambiguous situation is a complex one that juxtaposes a combination of realities that are not only in apposition to each other but in opposition to each other as well. The nature of the opposition varies from logical incongruities and exceptions to the rule to conflicting moral axioms. All realms of existence participate in ambiguity, though Christian ethicists are most cognizant of the ambiguities of history and morality. Historical ambiguity usually denotes events that are inexplicable. In fact, to the extent that all events are unique and in that sense incongruous, they are ambiguous. The mysterious conjunction of divine providence, natural law, and human freedom is the primary locus of ambiguity from a Christian point of view.

Knowledge may also be ambiguous in the sense that elements of experience appear to be in contradiction even though plausible and compelling. Even the most obviously apparent truth is seldom simple; some experiences can thus be described only by use of paradox. With the Apostle Paul, we "see through a glass darkly" as we wait for a clearer vision of a higher synthesis than mortal existence allows. Fortunately, life permits a measure of suspended judgment, but as William James once insisted, some options, especially moral ones, are "forced, living and momentous." Response to the ambiguous is inevitable unless we opt out of life altogether. After all, there is something right and abundant about almost everything, and there is something wrong and stingy about almost everything.

Even certain Judeo-Christian institutions that are reported in Scripture as having been established by God are ambiguous and must, therefore, be radically reformed or abandoned. It was the unique calling of the prophets to expose the failure of such sacred cultic and religio-political practices as the judges, the monarchy, the sacrificial system, and temple worship. All of these were either sharply criticized or repudiated by the prophets, though having been instituted by God. As Gerhard von Rad once put it, "How often was it not God himself who drove Israel out of her religious heritage; how often was she called upon explicitly to 'remember not the former things, Isaiah 43:18 . . .' The radical nature of its (the prophet's) criticism and judgments and warning beggars all comparisons.... What we have here is at every point the inevitable struggle of revelation against the religion of revelation."[7]

Despite the prophet's penchant for exposing ambiguities, whether in the form of incompleteness, pretense or corruption, it is nevertheless more than one would normally expect for prophecy to turn against itself as, for example, in St. Paul's confession that "prophecies will cease" (1 Cor. 13:8). Hence, "is it not as if the whole religion of Israel is ground as between two millstones, between the Word of God which so definitely institutes and orders and forms it and the Word of God by which one must always say, every concrete obedience to his command is no less definitely unmasked as unbelief?"[8]

Our world is an ambiguous world as epistemologically, historically, morally, and religiously perceived. Retreat from knowledge into simple thought, into social enclaves, and into moral perfectionism in order to avoid ambiguity will at best bring temporary escape. Eventually we must face the fact that we are all caught between the upper and nether millstones. Yet, by God's grace, we may hope that the grist of our commitment to the common good in the name of Christ may not be turned simply into historical chaff. For out of the painful, grinding ambiguities of history, nourishing sustenance may be produced for the hungry of the world.

7 Gerhard von Rad, *Old Testament Theology*, vol. II, (New York: Harper, 1960), 381-2.
8 *Ibid.*, 382.

But it may be contended that the problem of Christian ethics as stated in my thesis is passé; that it belongs to an earlier period in Mennonite history and reflects an earlier mood, if not an early twentieth-century dependence upon an existential analysis of reality. The clear antithesis between the sect and the church, love and justice, church and world, weakness and strength, nonresistance and nonviolence, functional poverty and wealth is no longer where Mennonites are, so it is claimed.

To be sure, the language of Mennonites has changed with their social situation. Now at least some Mennonites know that they are out there in the world. Simultaneously, business is no longer condemned because it is competitive. Mennonite Economic Development Associates has seen to that by suggesting how Mennonites can do business "with a difference." And didn't John Howard Yoder somehow legitimate politics as a Christian category in *The Politics of Jesus* (1972), and has justice not been given biblical legitimacy by renewed study of the Old Testament prophets as well as by the appeal of liberation theologies? And how can Mennonites be against institutions while having so many? And surely, Mennonites cannot be against life insurance. Now they sell it while calling it "mutual aid." And we can no longer be against wealth: Mennonite millionaires support Mennonite colleges.

Not many years ago, Mennonite colleges and seminaries rejected endowments in principle. That was when they had none and could get along without any. Now they launch large endowment campaigns for many millions. None of us want to be "legalists" any more. Indeed, in Charles Scriven's *The Transformation of Culture* purported to reflect contemporary Anabaptist thinking, killing a criminal is defended.[9] To deny the right to kill the killer of children playing in a California playground is said to be "legalistic," and who wants to be legalistic? But isn't this the argument for the "just war" in miniature?

Discipleship

With regard to discipleship, which according to the Anabaptist Vision is the essence of Christianity, we still talk about it but its content is becoming vague. In the 1950s discipleship, especially with the help of Bonhoeffer's *Cost of Discipleship*, stood for "rigorous imitation." Obviously, imitation can mean different things. But we were pretty sure what it meant for us: we acknowledged that the "gate" was narrow and few will go in. And we were sure that discipleship, while presupposing commitment, *agape*, conversion, and an obedient attitude, must be measured by concrete acts.

9 Charles Scriven, *The Transformation of Culture: Christian Social Ethics after H. Richard Niebuhr* (Scottdale, Pa.; Kitchener, Ont.: Herald Press, 1988).

But in recent years, we are less sure what shape discipleship should take. At least, the Mennonite Church no longer insists upon discipleship in its radical forms. The gate has been widened. Now Mennonites may be rich with impunity. They may divorce and remarry, go deeply into debt, wear fancy clothes, drive expensive cars, use bill collectors, sue at law, own many farms, accept government doles, stay at fancy hotels, and still be disciples. Somehow, the "eye of the needle" is larger than it used to be. Maybe that is why discipleship is most recently referred to as "solidarity" with Jesus, whatever that may mean concretely, rather than literally "following after." Some Mennonites today almost jump with joy when an ethicist such as Stanley Hauerwas tells us that we should look away from quandaries and concentrate upon character building and community formation, while Walter Wink tells us that Jesus really didn't mean for his followers to turn the other cheek and go the second mile out of a submissive spirit. Rather, Jesus was trying to shame his accusers. And the Lord's sayings are being made less offensive by interpreting them as Jewish wisdom literature. If recent literary criticism does not allow sufficient leverage to redefine faithfulness, let it be known that the Sermon on the Mount, in its rigorous embodiment, applied to the first generation or so, but not now. As noted economist Paul Samuelson once put it, "If you cannot deliver pie in the sky, you redefine the pie." Or to use another analogy, "If you can no longer win by the rules of four hundred years, you change the rules."

It is quite possible that my more traditional, Old Mennonite perfectionistic interpretation of Jesus' ethic is more philosophical than recent biblical criticism would support. But my rather literalist interpretation corresponds roughly with the classical tradition which, even before Constantine, saw in Jesus a perfectionistic ethic which could not be embodied socially except in correlation with, or dialectically related to, other normative structures such as the Ten Commandments and natural law.

I cannot escape the "extraordinary" (*perisson*, Matt. 5:47) character of Jesus' demands. Perfectionism is patterned in the Gospels; it is not occasional or accidental. Jesus simply did not feel it necessary to qualify his ethic in order to reduce its offense and to make it work. If he had conceded that normal sexual development would inevitably lead an adolescent to look at least once at an attractive woman to lust after her; if he had acknowledged that one could be anxious but should not be "overly anxious" about the future; if he had conceded that in some cases divorce may be allowed for more defensible reasons than "hardness of heart"; if he had commended a widow who gave all she had except enough for her children's supper; then appeals to the reasonableness of Jesus might let us off the hook. But Jesus made no such concessions, presumably because of his conception of the nature of God the Father and because of the eschaton. In other words, because God is love, and the time is short.

My problem with contemporary tendencies is that as Mennonites become assimilated, Jesus is domesticated according to demand. Jesus is simply being watered down. As long as they enjoyed the security of farm land, they could reject life insurance out of regard for filial trust, declaring life insurance to be worldly. But when Mennonites entered professional and business enterprise, life insurance became a necessity. Because it became a necessity to do business in the world, it became no problem. Litigation was considered worldly–until Mennonites got into institutional and business life. Then it became all right in principle. Divorce and remarriage were condemned–until Mennonites began to divorce and remarry; then these actions not only came to be tolerated but were made "redemptive." What I resist is "sliding scale" discipleship–that is, discipleship redefined to reduce or remove the tension between the perfectionistic ideal and contemporary reality. Jesus "cannot be dysfunctional," it is claimed. Therefore, Jesus must have meant what makes sense to us.

At a conference held several years ago on economics Mennonite economists, theologians, and businessmen presented learned papers on Mennonite economics without mentioning *agape* love once, while justice was explicitly advocated as the operating principle of "Christian" enterprise.[10] No mention was made of the tension between *suum quique* [justice: to each their due] and *agape* needing to be bridged. *Agape* was simply dropped without even acknowledging its loss. It seems that after having been against justice as a Christian category for some four hundred years, Mennonites, upon accepting justice uncritically, are in reality dropping their commitment to *agape* by default as a matter of convenience. They are abandoning the extraordinary in exchange for the ordinary, or abandoning what Luther called "evangelical" righteousness for "civil" righteousness as set forth classically by natural law, and without acknowledging the significance of their action.

What impresses me is the uncritical ease with which Mennonites today trade off controlling categories of traditional ethics when they appear to pose difficulties with practical life. To be sure, it is easier conceptually to exchange one category for another than to hold them in dialectical tension. No one enjoys conflict, especially when dealing with issues of ultimate concern.

But how else can one be true to the tradition and constructively involved in the world at the same time? In the typical social situation one has to shift gears from policy to policy and even from moment to moment. When there are gears to be shifted, despite occasional grinding, good drivers have maximum control of the vehicle. Far better than to rely on the deceptive simplicity of fluid drive, as any car buff, race driver, or driver of an institutional eighteen-wheeler would attest. If Mennonites want to get into business and dabble in politics and institutional life, they had better adopt a mind-set of dialectics in which neither love nor justice stand alone or are exchangeable but rather interact as distinct yet related

10 "Anabaptist/Mennonite Faith and Economics: Breaking The Silence," Conrad Grebel College, Waterloo, Ontario, Mar. 24-27, 1990.

principles. For example, when justice is tempered by mercy, mercy is disciplined by justice, compassion is structured by law, law is softened by compassion, nonresistance is socialized by non-violent resistance, and peaceful resistance is restrained by nonresistant inclinations.

The problem of undialectical ethics is the tendency to absolutize the relative. Unless Mennonite businessmen are prepared to accept as their final norm the same ethic that informs General Motors and Westinghouse, they must bring justice, which is always relative, under the judgment of sacrificial love. In so doing, they will attach the adjective "Christian" sparingly to their operations, in recognition of the fact that their "just" policies are more likely to express the balance of worldly pressures than the purity of altruistic love.

Mennonites continue to talk about discipleship and Anabaptism almost ad nauseum, but much of it is loose talk. For Mennonite discipleship language is no longer backed up in the communal consciousness by the gold standard of Jesus' sayings as rigorous, sacrificial, "upside down," extraordinary, impractical Sermon on the Mount presuppositions. Discipleship language these days generally refers to something between the extraordinariness of Jesus' ethic and the everyday reasonableness of civil righteousness. At the same time, emphasis has shifted from observable concrete actions to motive, intention, and character.

To redefine *agape* essentially as motive can be quite misleading apart from a fairly definite determination of what is acceptable and unacceptable conduct. To shift the focus from act to intention undialectically is dangerous, since such a transposition can too easily dispense with the radical implications of discipleship and can lead to almost anything. Even wars may be fought with the best of intentions. We cannot avoid the "offense" of Jesus' radicality, because, like Everest for the mountain climber, Jesus' ethic for the Christian is there. Hence we must decide what to do with an "impossible" ethic or, as Reinhold Niebuhr put it more positively, the "impossible possibility."

Surely, every religious tradition does and indeed must revise its theology and ethics from time to time. But the question is how to change with integrity. If the Mennonite Church defined discipleship in the 1950s univocally and made such a point of it that those questioning the adequacy thereof were disciplined, only to redefine discipleship a generation later, the least one would expect is an acknowledgement of a fundamental methodological shift. To put it bluntly, when discipleship was defined radically, the Mennonite Church assumed a difference between real disciples and ordinary Christians, disciples being those who are "faithful" and Christians being those who do some but not necessarily all of the "all things" of Matt. 28:20. Anabaptist-Mennonites do pretty much what good Lutherans and Presbyterians do, with the exception of going to war and holding public office. Still today we use the term "discipleship" to cover common ground. What does this mean? Can we still say that some are disciples and others are ordinary believers, or should we say that all are disciples, some more "faithful" than others, or that discipleship as a concept is so imprecise as to share the ambiguity of the term "Christian"? It would seem that in practice, discipleship and Christianity are becoming tautological, and that is serious for Mennonites in light of traditional claims. I am becoming more than slightly uncomfortable with the frequency and the unguarded use of terms like "discipleship" and "Anabaptism" when used to describe Mennonite middle class life in a democratic context of religious freedom such as ours.

Politics

What to do with an impossible ethic must be faced by everyone, even with reference to the family and business, but particularly with politics. Politics is a many-faceted thing, and responsibility for the political order may take many forms. To be sure, Mennonites have moved in the direction of political responsibility. Whereas Mennonites have been traditionally apolitical, with the civil rights struggles of the 1960s and the advent of liberation theologies, not to speak of minority demands for justice within the Mennonite Church, the Mennonite Church has moved from nonresistance to nonviolence and legitimated witness to government, calling it prophecy. In *The Politics of Jesus* (1974), John Howard Yoder presented Jesus as a political figure. But he did so without addressing the central issue, namely the problem of power. The title, *The Politics of Jesus,* is a euphemism in that politics, as the term is normally used, includes what Yoder rejects, namely participation in the actual formulation of law, legislation, and the enforcement thereof. While making a place for witness, Yoder makes no place in the life of the follower of Christ for real, earthly kingship or its modern democratic equivalent. To speak is finally "admissible," but not to govern.

I have only respect for prophets and prophecy. The development of personal and communal consciousness with respect to the public order is a great achievement of the prophetic tradition of Israel and of the emergence of democracy in the Western world. Under certain circumstances prophecy demands an extraordinary measure of courage; it may lead to suffering and death. For most people living in democratic nations, joining politics cannot go beyond talking as a private individual or by participating in organized parties and interest groups. I look back with considerable satisfaction upon my own involvement with the civil rights movement in the 1960s, including some time in jail. Upon the assassination of Martin Luther King, Jr., I was chosen by the President of Harvard University, along with several others, to address the University as it officially "came to order."

But the question is whether politics, given its ambiguity, can be a Christian vocation. By politics, I mean more than prophetic witness; I mean participation in government as a responsible decision maker, legislator, judge, department head, ambassador, or high-level executive for whom the holding of political office within a democracy is to be "accountable." The office holder must make hard decisions, many of them controversial and crucial in that the well-being of people is dependent upon them, and they are inevitably preferential. Further, politics is power politics by its very nature. Of course, politicians talk as well as act. But if their effectiveness is to be maximized, they must be prophets who speak, lawmakers who legislate, and officials who administer. They visualize better things and propose how to realize them. They put themselves on the line as few others in society do. They seldom go to sleep having accomplished their best intentions, and they inevitably struggle with problems of guilt. They are forced to deal with the world as it is while being motivated by dreams, possibly even such a utopian dream as the Kingdom of God.

Why enter politics? Certainly not for money or personal glory. Generally speaking, there is no money in politics, and the glory is ephemeral. No professional is more scrutinized these days than the public servant. Indeed, politics is often cruel. The reason Christians would go into politics is to find leverage for good. One would go into politics for the same reason one would go to Somalia to do relief work under MCC. One does so to serve the neighbor–the neighbor being human beings who benefit by the ministry of just laws, humane structures, imaginative policies, and enlightened diplomacy. In an interconnected world like ours, neighbors are not simply those whom one knows personally, but people belonging to certain categories or classes who need to be helped in the aggregate. People are loved, however imperfectly, through policies as well as through personal relations. The prophets of the Old Testament observed widows, orphans, and the poor who were treated unjustly. I trust that they shared personally what they had with them. But they are remembered because of their appeals to the nation and to the king for structural changes. The genius of western democracies is that channels are open to anyone who would lead in the development of public consciousness through the enactment of just laws which, with time, become traditions of justice. For some people, the only love they know is the minimal, indirect, refracted love expressed by food stamps, public housing, and police protection.

Obviously, not everyone will be called to enter politics. But politics cannot be ignored as if it could be placed in a category less fundamental to human existence than those of food, water, air, and family. Politics is a presupposition of life. Mennonite refugees surely must know that. Politics is part of the climate within which we all live: it is the difference between order and disorder, freedom and slavery, life and death. Virtually all of life is political. A cup of cold water in New York City is political water. We may say with the prophet Amos, "Let justice roll down like waters and righteousness like a mighty stream" (Amos 5:24). But justice does not roll down like waters. It is piped, and piping systems are unbelievably intricate. The choice of the source of water, its channeling, pumping, purifying, distribution, pricing, and bill collecting are all political. So is transportation, electricity, medical care, police protection, Social Security, regulation of financial exchanges, sanitation, sewage disposal, and legal defences of free institutions, including organized religion. Democracy at its best provides the ubiquity of politics and freedom for everyone to live out religious and metaphysical commitments at the same time. The genius of liberal democracy is its capacity to support life without excessively controlling it.

Even Mennonite colleges, mental health institutions, and nursing homes get a significant portion of their operating income from public sources, albeit indirectly. Ever since the "Great Society" of U.S. President Lyndon Johnson, virtually all senior Mennonites have come to depend for their living on Social Security and Medicare (and their Canadian equivalents). Some former Mennonite bishops, having exhausted their resources, are entirely dependent upon the state for their support. These days church support at best supplements public support, not vice versa. This represents a fundamental shift from the depression days of the 1930s, when Mennonites rejected "relief" for theological and communal reasons.

Mennonite reluctance to enter politics is sometimes based upon the assumption that to be actively engaged in politics is to invest one's energies outside of the church. That is, in regard to the commitment of time, energies, obligations, subtle commitments of loyalty, and psychic and communal orientations, church-world "two masters" considerations should pull in only one direction–toward the church. But this is the kind of argument that Mennonites have used against almost all commitments and attachments outside the church, employing it to resist education, business, art, and the practice of law. The jury is still out on whether Mennonite identity can be retained in light of Mennonite participation in modern pluralism. However, at least selective involvement in politics, while admittedly ambiguous, needs to be no greater threat to church life than some other more subtle extraneous commitments.

A major consideration is motivation. If Mennonites were to enter politics consciously, explicitly, and sacrificially in order to serve humanity rather than for reasons of self-serving pride, they could see politics as a "missionary field." Obviously, such service would not, indeed dare not, be seen as an extension of the institutional church. But it may be in line with one of the major concerns of the church, namely, human betterment. If all Mennonites would normally give all of their time and energies to the church as monastics do or even as Hutterites may, then the either-or "to what will you give your life" argument would be conclusive. But as long as Mennonites give forty hours per week or more to their professions and are still considered committed members of the church, possibly a few Mennonite politicians could do the same.

Sometimes it is argued that the redemptive purposes of God are accomplished through the church and not through the public sphere. I agree that the church as the body of Christ has a special relationship to God, and that one's commitment to office holding is optional and relative to particular circumstances. So far as my theology is concerned, I believe that the role of the Christian in politics is simply humanitarian. One tries to help the public to achieve some sort of reasonable order which may be said to be Christian only to the extent that honesty, decency, fairness, civility, stability, hope, and neighborliness are Christian. The political order is not the Kingdom of God and, of course, neither is the church. To press Kingdom ethics upon pluralistic democratic order is not only unlikely of success but wrong. We should not assume that religious consensus, Christian or otherwise, is the basis for political life. But a lot can be done in the political sphere, without Kingdom pretensions, that points in the direction of the Kingdom of God.

I will not set forth here a theology of the state, except to insist upon minimal expectations of governments. The primary function of government is to maintain order by the moderate use of enlightened force. Insofar as modern governments support health and human services of many kinds, the operating principle of their regulation is justice. Occasionally governments may prudently go the second, enlightened, mile. Their self-interest may include the forgiveness of international debts, and they may rehabilitate educable criminals as expressions of humanity. But their most generous inclinations should not be construed as Christian ethics. The humanity of government may reflect the ethic of Christ, but it may not directly and necessarily proceed from Christian faith.

The tendency today to ground Christian witness to the state in biblical theology, by transposing ancient theocratic presuppositions to modern secular democratic processes, can be misguided if not dangerous. To propose that the state can be expected to be in effect Christian because Jesus is Lord, and to draw from that presupposition that the sword is ill-advised because it is sinful per se (a supposed implication of the cosmic rule of a nonviolent Christ), fails to take into consideration the fact that the Ascension has as yet transformed neither humankind nor beast. Unfortunately, the lion does not lie down with the lamb, and the human situation, though reformed in some respects, is hardly transformed. The Christian community still waits for the transformation of "all things" when God will be "all in all."

Politics, whether in the form of elective legislative office or appointed bureaucratic service, should be explored by Mennonites for theological-humane reasons–not just tolerated for the less spiritually motivated. Surely God cares what happens in the political realm, since it is there that millions upon millions of people are supported or victimized. And with respect to peacemaking, since we have now moved from nonresistance to nonviolent resistance, why not move on to peacemaking with "portfolio," i.e., with political power? With the Quakers we must "speak to power with love." But cannot some Mennonites also "speak to power with power?" Sometimes it is possible to make peace as nonparticipants in the power arena. As Mennonites, we are trying to become organized mediators these days. Disinterested peace mediation should certainly be encouraged, and "peacemaker teams" may help. But frequently the most effective peace processes are those carried out by participants in diplomatic services. Some of the greatest peacemaking public servants of this century have been people like Gorbachev, Genscher (the Foreign Minister of Germany), Willy Brandt, UN Secretary de Cuellar, Nobel Prize winner Oscar Arias (President of Costa Rica) and, if we may extend the concept of peacemaking to domestic politics, Surgeon General C. Everett Koop in the politics of health, and many U.S. mayors who are among the most reviled these days as they preside over disintegrating cities. Are these not among the most courageous men and women of our age?

Of course, not all so-called public servants are really servants. Many are selfish and corrupt, and politics is partisan at best. But apart from a death wish, what more unselfish sacrifice is there than to risk one's sanity, if not one's life, as have these and other political figures? With all due respect to Mother Teresa, whom we should honor and revere, she has a less morally ambiguous burden and, in that respect, a lesser one than does the mayor of a major city. Those who bathe the dying can do no wrong. Those who administer city governments can do no right, so it seems.

I would additionally suggest that public servants are not necessarily "outside the perfection of Christ" simply because they are "magistrates." Being inside or outside the perfection of Christ cannot be determined arbitrarily by church affiliation and vocation as with Schleitheim. It is not determined by communal affiliation or moral perfection as such. Being inside the perfection of Christ is determined by a multitude of considerations, such as the quality of one's decisions, one's personal attachment to Christ, and the appropriation of God's grace. I am not happy with the term "perfection of Christ" when used to refer to inclusion or exclusion based upon moral qualifications. One can be of the "world" even as a Mennonite Church leader in good standing, and one can, by the grace of God, I trust, be a member of Christ's body as a mayor or a secretary of state. We are, of course, assuming active church membership in any case.

Obviously, if one were to accept responsibility for the social order as a general attitude toward society, as I do, and yet remain a pacifist in full fellowship with the Mennonite Church, practical and theoretical problems abound.

Public acceptance is one of the problems. Is the public prepared to elect a pacifist to public office? My impression is that were one to (1) define pacifism openly as a personal calling while allowing that the state may, indeed must, use police and at least a minimum of military force to fulfill its function; and (2) devote energies to peacemaking in particular by advancing the most rational, imaginative, inexpensive, minimal uses of force, the response of the public would not be automatically negative. With Gorbachev we entered into a new period of history characterized by the reduction of arms in line with peacemaking consonant with order. Today, peacemaking, like medicine, must increasingly become preventative. Now since Mennonites, after some four hundred years, have approved prophecy in the context of the nation, they would do well to move on to office-holding. Both are essential to collective life.

Prophecy without political accountability is incomplete. If grace without discipleship is cheap, as Bonhoeffer says, so is justice without accountable participation. What right has one to prophesy without accepting responsibility for decision making, management, and accountability? Of course, some prophets are stoned, but in a democracy most prophets suffer little–sometimes it is even fashionable to prophesy, especially in so-called liberal circles. Sitting on the sidelines and complaining is legal and indeed helpful if one is on the right side of the issues. Monday morning quarterbacking is all that most of us can do anyway. But to complain about how things are run, while refusing as a matter of principle to manage them, is less than forthcoming.

Ultimately the question boils down to whether Christians should feel responsible for the outcome of history. I use the term "feel" instead of a more instrumental verb since no one person or group can alone be responsible for the outcome of history. To feel responsible translates into doing all one can to steer history in the most positive direction possible. John Howard Yoder, however, declares that Christians should not accept responsiblity for the outcome of history. He reinforces his position by the obvious fact that you can never know how history will turn out. Personally, I cannot divorce myself so categorically from historical outcomes because to do so seems to me to be unloving and uncaring. The outcome of history is the outcome of the neighbor; to love one's neighbor is to care for the neighbor's history. And when it comes to outcomes, what outcomes in life are ever certain? Not even the outcome of one's self, let alone one's children, is ever known with certainty. To leave destinies up to God may sound pious, but that is not the way we treat those whom we love.

Compromise

Certainly one of the most controversial terms in my ethical vocabulary is the word "compromise." I wish that I could find a less loaded word for what I mean. Suffice it to say, compromise, as I use the term, refers to the failure to actualize pure love perfectly, and that is the main problem of Christian social ethics. But only through compromise can love be objectified socially, however imperfectly. Love is extended through compromise as it is allayed with elements which may be the natural consequence of existence in this kind of created order, not to speak of historical contingency. When love is combined with aggressive power, constitutional limits, legal regulations, prudential policies, competitive pressures, conservative establishments, and evolutionary differentiations, it is enhanced in that it becomes effective in corporate systems, but compromised in that its character is changed in so far as it tends to become defensive and preferential.

Take Mennonite Mutual Aid, for example. It started out in response to the most simple communal impulses to help those in need with a minimum of protective fine print. But it has in the meantime grown into a life insurance company in competition with secular institutions and subject to much the same laws, accounting and fiduciary principles, investment policies, and exclusionary practices as most insurance companies. But it is effective, and as Mennonites we should support it. Even so, MMA compromises. Only through compromise can it function; its corporate structure requires compromise. If you want to know what goes on at MMA, at Goshen College, and among Mennonite businesses at their best, consider an amalgam of "Christian" virtues such as love, patience, longsuffering, grace, self-denial, generosity, nonjudgmental acceptance, turning the other cheek, and transforming power juxtaposed dialectically in combination with classical "natural" virtues such as justice, assertive power, legal defenses, self-regarding impulses, ontological realism, and reforming change. Such are the ways of the world at their best. Compromise in its social embodiment is love diffused and amalgamated with "worldly," civil virtues. It is the combination of "heavenly" and "earthly" virtues by which the grace of God is spread abroad, albeit under the conditions of historical-natural existence. Compromise is the term used in connection with "ambiguous" love. It is a condition that is good–but not entirely good in all respects and not necessarily good for everyone.

Of course, compromise can easily degenerate into a destructive alliance with evil. Compromise is destructive when it reinforces wrong purposes and when the moral expense is out of proportion to the good that is done. When compromised inordinately, love becomes selfishness, justice injustice, power oppression, order dominance, establishment idolatry, hierarchy privilege, office self-justification, and the conditioned claims to be the unconditioned. When that happens, the Christian answer is to dissent and to be nonconformed, and even to separate. To place compromise on a continuum of ambiguity as the subject matter for ethics is a function of the "discerning community." Where to draw the line is the issue. Different times, different circumstances, different identities obviously will bring different answers.[11]

Grace

The Christian community, while enjoying the power of enabling grace in lifestyles embodying various manners of discipleship, will nevertheless in its more mature moments acknowledge that life in this world can be sustained only by God's forgiving grace. Even the most radical of disciples will, upon reflection, rejoice not in moral achievements but in the fact that his or her "name

11 See J. Lawrence Burkholder, "The Peace Churches as Communities of Discernment," *The Christian Century*, Sept. 4, 1963: 1072-75. I believe that I was the first to introduce the idea of discernment as a structural element of Christian ethics into Mennonite thinking. It should be recognized that Christian social ethics presupposes the integrity, independence, and faith of the Christian community, especially of the congregational level.

is written in heaven." Hence, the theological predication of classical doctrines of justification by faith, the objective atonement, fallen creation, original sin and eternal hope. It is too much to ascribe to discipleship the place it has in "the Anabaptist Vision," for there it is declared to be the essence of Christianity. If the author had declared discipleship to have been "of" the essence, I would have no objection. Indeed, for Harold Bender to place discipleship in opposition to the evangelical tradition of justification, he may have made a legitimate point against an over-emphasis of, not to speak of defective uses of, *sola fide*. But the ensuing Gospel fails to take seriously the depth and persistence of sin, and the existentialist plight of human beings in relation to the eternal God. The Anabaptist Vision refuses to acknowledge the tragic side of life from which the purest of saints and the greatest of moral adventurers need to be saved. After all, we are all caught in the subtleties of sin and the ambiguities of existence.

Having been given a measure of Christ's transforming grace, I nevertheless continue to struggle introspectively with the consciousness of good and evil in my life. I trust that my experience of *Anfechtungen* is not of the depth and intensity of Luther's, but I can at least sympathize with Luther and put the best of interpretations upon his doctrine of *simul justus et peccator*. Indeed, if I may be said to be an Anabaptist (as I trust I am), I feel more like a Luther than a Michael Sattler, closer to a Pilgram Marpeck than to a Conrad Grebel. As I have sometimes put it, I begin the day full of Christian intentionality as would an Anabaptist, devote myself to administration as would a Calvinist, and close the day asking for forgiveness as would a Lutheran. I am, some might say, a classical Protestant evangelical Anabaptist–unless my less dialectically-oriented Mennonite sisters and brothers would claim that no recourse to paradox could redeem such an obvious contradiction.

What I have looked for is a doctrine of grace that not only addresses the problems of personal sins, willfully committed, but also social sins, structurally necessitated. With respect to the former, the Anabaptist-Mennonite tradition has made admirable, possibly even unique, provision through communal processes of repentance, confession, and restoration. In that sense, Anabaptists and Mennonites may be said to be evangelical.

But what I find missing in Mennonite theology and experience is provision for unavoidable compromises attendant upon responsible involvement in worldly structures. And the moral limits imposed by systems of law, education, economics, health administration, agricultural policies, and especially politics. These are routinized, legalized, and institutionalized activities by which humanity is collectively organized and, to a measure, coerced. As a matter of rule, anyone who becomes involved in a responsible way participates in both the positive, life-giving aspects of structured existence and the negative aspects which are sinful. No matter how essential so-called "orders of creation" are, they not only operate on levels which accommodate sinful existence, but are organized on principles which extend the fall. This world is not organized as the

Kingdom of God would be. World orders make "honorable" provision for at least a measure of legalized selfishness, partisan pride, regional provincialism, national prejudice, and class privilege.

In a sense, Anabaptist-Mennonite theology has acknowledged structural sin, though in a negative way. The interconnection of fallen structures was implied by the authors of the Schleitheim Confession when, with the generic significance attributed to the "magistracy," society generally was rejected as being "outside the perfection" of Christ. Hence, a purist theology and social strategy of radical separation.

As would be expected, such a Pelagian theological analysis and negative social bias freed Mennonites from the task of developing a social concept of grace. Of course, it may be said that the Anabaptists and Mennonites emphasized "enabling grace" where sheer human resolve and communal disciplines were in themselves deemed inadequate. But having limited their purview to personal and communal contexts, no need for "social grace" was perceived–though any objective analysis of Mennonite life would seem to call for an evangelical doctrine of collective grace. After all, those who feel they are really not of the world socially are not likely to feel impelled to seek forgiveness for being of the world ethically.

By contrast, despite my life of identification with the Mennonite Church, I have felt myself to be very much a part of the world. I simply have not been able to infer from my rather radical commitment to discipleship that my need for grace is of a different sort than the needs of industrialists, bankers, politicians, policemen, and soldiers. I too have participated in fallen orders, and I have benefited from their largess. Even when I have demurred, for conscience sake, from active involvement in compromising "service" such as law enforcement, I have felt the burden of guilt as if I had been an active participant. As president of Goshen College, having called the city police to defend students from intruders and thieves, I cannot separate myself from the "sinful" restraint of sin by armed police. I cannot fully assuage my conscience just because I did not personally enforce law and make peace by use of clubs and pistols. In a more general way, I feel involved in economic wars, environmental pollution, political injustice, and social malformations beyond acts of my own personal immediate culpability. And having survived World War II, I cannot but carry a measure of guilt for hoping that Hitler would be defeated even though I have no blood on my hands. After all, I fought against Hitler inwardly in spirit if not outwardly with arms.

Thus I have had to draw upon the Protestant doctrine of justification by faith to find grace sufficient to serve as a basis for socially responsible acts done and undone. I have found in the atonement the courage to undertake moral risks, at least up to the point where destroying life begins. Of course, I hope that anticipation of forgiveness for "positive" compromise is not tantamount to a presumption of grace. For while the doctrine of justification has been put to bad use as an excuse for sin, I feel called to draw upon its best articulation for good use since the Anabaptist-Mennonite concept of grace is inadequate. "Sin bravely" means to me the privilege, indeed the duty, to help bear the burdens of God's world, knowing full well that my hands will not be without the stains of social sin. My moral sense, having been enlivened by the Anabaptist Vision, is kindly assuaged by a doctrine of grace as developed by Augustine and the Reformers.

Surely no more rigorous demand for obedient discipleship has ever been uttered than by Jesus when he said, "When you have done everything you were told to do . . . say, we are unworthy servants; we have only done our duty" (Luke 17:10). How else shall we interpret this statement than as the ground for a doctrine of grace as expansive as the world itself (John 3:16)?

V

In these autobiographical reflections I have attempted to set forth the problem of social responsibility from the Mennonite perspective. This has involved not only an analysis of contemporary social policy of the Mennonites but also a study of the most significant theological ideas upon which Mennonite social policy rests–especially the idea of discipleship and the idea of the church.

In conclusion, I wish to underscore the fundamental conflict in which Mennonites are involved. It is the conflict between a professed ethical absolutism in the form of nonresistance, the "way of the cross," the simple life and the relativities of the social order. Traditionally Mennonites have assumed that this conflict could be resolved by retreat into the simplicities of semi-independent agrarian communities. In recent years, however, (especially within the past fifteen years), cultural isolation has become impossible. Industrial and technical revolutions have been invading Mennonite communities at an alarming rate. As a result, the community life of Mennonites has changed drastically. The simplicity, independence, and mutuality of their lives have been replaced to a considerable extent by the complexity, bureaucracy, interdependence, "other-directedness," and power struggle of society.

Undoubtedly an objective analysis of traditional Mennonite life would indicate that relations within the Mennonite community have never been totally separated from the evils of world culture. However, the social and economic revolutions of modern times, which have turned the basically agrarian economy into a highly organized industrial and technical society, are challenging Mennonite ethics in much the same way that the thought of Ernst Troeltsch and Reinhold Niebuhr was challenged earlier. The question which Troeltsch and Niebuhr asked was, How can Christ's absolute ethic of love become relevant to the structure of modern life? Troeltsch asked it in the face of the Marxian interpretation of social dynamics, and Niebuhr asked it in the context of economic conflict in Detroit in the 1920s. Both came to the conclusion that the love ethic of Christ cannot be applied directly to the affairs of society. This is not to deny the relevance of the Gospel for the economic and political realms. It does mean, however, that the Gospel ethic cannot be applied as an operative principle. The result has been a revolution in ethics comparable to the revolution in society.

In the light of this development (assuming that Mennonites will not pull out of the modern social ethos), the question arises whether they will be forced to reconsider their traditional social policy. My conviction is that the present crisis in Mennonite life will require a revision of the present Mennonite approach to society. This is not to suggest that Mennonites should consider "selling out" to world culture because of the intrinsic difficulties of embodying the ethic of Christ in the power arena, but to suggest that they must seek their traditional goals of brotherhood, peace, and mutuality under the conditions of compromise. Mennonites must realize that they are a part of the world system, that they share the guilt and responsibility for corporate evil, and that their attempts to be obedient to Christ and be the true church must take into consideration the ambiguities of their actual situation. This realistic approach will prevent perfectionistic illusions and despair.

Specifically, a place must be made in Mennonite ethics for power. Traditionally the Mennonite position has assumed that Christians can live without the exercise of power–that is, power in the form of compulsion and force. It may be agreed that, given the ideal combination of saintliness and simplicity, a small Christian society can live with a minimum amount of power. But certainly business organizations, educational institutions, and even highly organized mutual aid societies cannot operate by the pure principles of the love feast. All institutions are to a certain degree political in character, even though the service motive and personal piety can mitigate the political principle. For this reason Mennonites must re-examine the validity of nonresistance as a comprehensive norm for all Christian relations. It is my view that if nonresistance were actually practiced as an absolute principle, it would literally take Christians out of this world. A practical alternative would be nonviolent resistance as an approximation of the absolute ideal, which affords at the same time an opportunity to participate in the ambiguous struggles for justice in society.

Further, the Mennonite ethic must be reconsidered from the standpoint of its complete neglect of justice as a Christian goal. As stated earlier, justice has virtually no place in the Mennonite vocabulary. This has led to confusion as well as social apathy. It has left Mennonites without a word to describe the vast majority of their dealings with each other, since justice is the basic norm of economic life. The most unfortunate result of this neglect is, however, the tendency to shy away from the social problems of the world where justice, rather than pure love, characterizes both the method and the goal of social action. It is true that the Mennonite emphasis on love has had the advantage of going straight to the heart of the Christian ethic. However, it is a fact of social existence that love must take the form of justice if it is to be effective.

But before the practical decision can be made regarding the extent of Mennonite participation in society, certain prior decisions must be made on the level of hermeneutics. Today Mennonite biblical hermeneutics are in an uncertain state. To thoughtful Mennonites it is no longer clear, for example, just how literally Jesus' commands are to be kept. It is uncertain which of his commands are binding, and whether the relation of the church to society in the New Testament is normative for all later periods. It is uncertain whether the ethic of Jesus and the ethic of Paul are basically the same, and to what extent the Old Testament may be used as a guide for Christian conduct. The problem of social responsibility is baffling, not only because of the universally admitted practical difficulty of knowing how to influence society but also because Mennonites (like many other groups) are not certain of their presuppositions. Until Mennonites produce a system of ethics which will wrestle both with the essentials of Christianity and the realities of modern life, no final solution to this problem will be possible.

Despite these uncertainties, it is my conviction that some of the peculiar practices and theological emphases of Mennonites should be continued and actually extended. Emphasis upon nonconformity to the world should be emphasized, especially in view of the current tendency toward mass conformity. The tendency of the universal church to identify itself uncritically with the prevailing culture must be counterbalanced by the sectarian emphasis upon obedience to Christ. Over against the growing institutional character of church life, Mennonites may witness to the place of Christian brotherhood in the life of the church. In the area of social service, the unique personal ministry of Mennonites to human suffering in the form of voluntary relief and rehabilitation service should be multiplied. The most difficult area of Mennonite life, the area of peace education, also opens before Mennonites an overwhelming responsibility, especially in view of the atomic crisis. It must be assumed that greater interest in social and political affairs should not displace those attitudes and practices which were authentically Christian and which lie most closely to the eternal life of the Church of Christ.

In view of modern, dynamic, social pluralism, the time is probably past for comprehensive and final social policies. At best, Mennonites can formulate a general policy for the future which will be kept flexible at many points for the guidance of the Holy Spirit.

II

Burkholder and Beyond: Essays in Conversation

J. Lawrence Burkholder: Sectarian Realist

Rodney J. Sawatsky

I

The Anabaptist-Mennonite tradition is essentially sectarian–not in a pejorative sense but as Ernst Troeltsch used the term, to refer to a Christian community committed to living according to the perfectionistic love of Jesus Christ as defined in the Gospels.[1]

Throughout most of Christian history sectarianism is paralleled by, in tension with, even symbiotically related to, two other impulses: the churchly and the mystical or cultic. Leaving aside the mystical/cultic for now, the churchly is considered by Anabaptists and Mennonites as an illegitimate compromise with society and culture. The "fall" of the "church," epitomized by Constantine's embrace of Christianity in 313 AD, was and is the rejection of suffering love as normative for the faithful community of disciples in favor of a Christendom premised on the coercive sword and on an inclusive baptism.

These types–church and sect–are, however, ideal constructs only, analytically and heuristically invaluable yet always limited by historical reality. And historical reality for Anabaptists and Mennonites, as for most sectarians, is not accidental but essential. After all, the Incarnation was a concrete historical event within time and space. The disciples were called to leave all and follow, and were taught to be perfect even as their heavenly Father is perfect. Only those who lost their lives in following would find life. Suffering and even death may well be the lot of those who would be saved. All this and much more was taught and lived by Jesus of Nazareth within history. So too the faithful church in continuity with the Jesus of history is to continue the Incarnation within the complexities of history as the very body of Christ.

Though history is necessary for the sect, it is rather unkind to sectarianism. The sect is an idealistic, rather utopian construct, whereas history insists on realism. H. Richard Niebuhr, who continued Troeltsch's analysis, argued that the corrosive forces of historical reality almost invariably transmuted sects into less exclusive denominations.[2] Some sociologists challenged Niebuhr and produced examples, including some Mennonite, which remained sectarian over

Rodney J. Sawatsky is the President of Messiah College, Grantham, Pa.

1 Ernst Troeltsch, *The Social Teaching of the Christian Churches* (Chicago: University of Chicago Press, 1981).

2 H. Richard Niebuhr, *The Social Sources of Denominationalism* (New York: World Publishing Co., 1971).

many generations. Yet these same sociologists joined in documenting the acculturation and even the assimilation of Mennonites into the dominant culture and away from separatism. History with its ambiguities, contradictions, tragedies–that is, with its full embrace of human limitation and sin–cannot help but set road blocks to sectarian idealism.

Perhaps the reality of history challenges sectarianism particularly with the relativity of history. Human beings create history, but history also creates or cultivates being human. Cultures, societies, worldviews, and religions are socially or historically constructed. The clear word of God amidst the cacophonous words of humanity is thus at best heard or, to change the metaphor, seen "through a glass darkly." Historical reality tends more to relativize than to clarify the right and good at any particular time and place.

Yet sectarians cannot retreat from history. By entering history Christ pronounced history good, and challenged Christians to work out their faith in fear and trembling within the relativities of historical reality. The Christian problem, then, is not only lacking the will to act upon the right but also knowing the right even when we have the will. Being perfect, which is the sectarian challenge, is most difficult amidst the ambiguities of history. Nevertheless it is precisely within history where the church as a community and each individual Christian are called to follow the Way.

Few Mennonites have openly, systematically, and consistently confronted this sectarian dilemma. J. Lawrence Burkholder is a rare exception. Throughout much of his career he has been a rather lone voice for sectarian realism. While certainly influenced by the Christian realism school, especially of the brothers Niebuhr–Reinhold and H. Richard–the chastening of his sectarianism, even as their liberalism was chastened, largely resulted from historical experience and reflection on it. While seeking to fully account for historical realities, he did not abandon sectarianism. The two remain for him in tension, or in paradox, but neither is rejected in order to resolve the dilemma. He is a sectarian realist.

Lest anyone question this characterization of Burkholder, his own words provide clear evidence. This "sectarian realist" position is definitively articulated in the last two pages of his published doctoral dissertation, *The Problem of Social Responsibility from the Perspective of the Mennonite Church:*

> Mennonites must realize that they are a part of the world system and that they share the guilt and responsibility for corporate evil and that their attempts to be obedient to Christ and "be" the true church must take into consideration the "ambiguities" of their actual situation. This realistic approach will prevent perfectionistic illusions and despair.[3]

3 J. Lawrence Burkholder, *The Problem of Social Responsibility from the Perspective of the Mennonite Church* (Elkhart, Indiana: Institute of Mennonite Studies, 1989), 223.

This realism is balanced with a warm embrace of key sectarian themes. Burkholder is convinced that:

> . . . some of the peculiar practices of Mennonites should be continued and actually extended. Emphasis upon nonconformity to the world should be emphasized, especially in view of the current tendency to mass conformity. The tendency of the universal church to identify itself uncritically with the prevailing culture must be counterbalanced by the sectarian emphasis upon obedience to Christ. Over against the growing institutional character of church life, Mennonites may witness to the place of Christian brotherhood in the life of the church. In the area of social service, the unique personal ministry of Mennonites to human suffering in the form of voluntary relief and rehabilitation service should be multiplied. The most difficult area of Mennonite life, the area of peace education, also opens before Mennonites an overwhelming responsibility, especially in view of the atomic crisis. It must be assumed that greater interest in social and political affairs should not displace those attitudes and practices which were authentically Christian and which lie most closely to the enternal life of the Church of Christ.[4]

This sectarian realist position was not the product of ivory tower theorizing. True, Burkholder was a pastor and a professor, but his experience as a relief and United Nations administrator provided the anvil on which much of his theory was hammered out. Reinhold Niebuhr chronicled his Detroit in *Leaves*.[5] India and China were Burkholder's Detroit, and his "Autobiographical Reflections" are his "Leaves." Fundamental is Burkholder's conviction that historical reality must be fully accounted for in an adequate ethic and theology. "The China years that followed became the crucible for my ethical thinking," he says. "I had never had a course in ethics; my ethics came directly out of the encounter between Mennonite radical idealism and reality."[6]

Burkholder's primary learning in this encounter was the "distinct difference between love in its simple purity and in its social and organizational refraction."[7] Pure love is *agape* as incarnated in Jesus and fully revealed on the cross. It is "disinterested love, unmixed with anticipated rewards, reciprocations, mutual gratification, and preferences based on merit."[8] It requires perfection: "Hence, Jesus reminded us 'If you love those who love you, what reward will you get? Are not the tax collectors doing that . . . Be perfect,

4 Burkholder, *The Problem of Social Responsibility*, 224, and "The Limits of Perfection: Autobiographical Reflections" in this volume, hereafter cited as "Reflections," 54.

5 Reinhold Niebuhr, *Leaves from the Notebook of a Tamed Cynic* (New York: Richard R. Smith, 1930).

6 "Reflections," 6.

7 *Ibid.*, 8.

8 *Ibid.*

(i.e. indiscriminate) therefore, as your heavenly father is perfect.'"[9]

However, historical reality taught Burkholder "that such love is an historical possibility but it is at best an occasional one since it cannot be structured without contradiction." In contrast to Reinhold Niebuhr, the ideal is not impossible. Yet its possibility is limited. As for Niebuhr, the problem for Burkholder is focused in structures, which are of the essence for community. Even if the individual in isolation may be moral, society is inevitably less moral when measured against *agape*. "An important implication of the absoluteness of *agape* is that *agape* love cannot be structured unambiguously, for structure itself generally defenses, includes self-regarding implications, safeguards, lines of exclusion and sanctions." "Life, especially collective life, could not be run by pure *agape* alone. *Agape* may, however, serve as an ideal point of reference. It may invade the give-and-take of power structures under ad hoc circumstances but not on a continuous basis. *Agape* punctuates, but does not constitute, organized life." In sum, history taught Burkholder "the difference between the ethics of personal relations and corporate responsibilities."[10]

His autobiographical reflections detail this difference. Experience taught Burkholder that *agape* love and power and complexity were in conflict. Real "moral dilemmas," indeed "tragic necessity," resulted in the realization of the essential difference between nonresistance as a principle when applied to personal interests alone and when the welfare of other people are concerned as well, or when he ate and those outside his door starved, or in his role of "dividing" for the benefit of the ninety-nine rather than the one according to rules, policies, and procedures rather than in freedom. Says Burkholder: "In general, I came to associate the private sphere with spontaneity, compassion, sacrifice, perfectionistic possibilities, and the public sphere was the place of social effectiveness. Gradually, 'to be good' and 'to get something done' came into tension if not outright conflict."[11]

The exercise of power over others,[12] the omnipresence of ambiguity and the necessity of compromise,[13] "the reality . . . of the depth and persistence of systematic evil, the frailty of human flesh, and the ravages of nature"[14], all this and more, for Burkholder, is the real world. Yet for the Christian simply to look to Jesus as normative cannot resolve these real world difficulties, because Jesus was not limited as we are. When Jesus faced a shortage of food, for example, he

9 *Ibid.*, 9.
10 *Ibid.*, 8-10.
11 *Ibid.*, 11-16.
12 *Ibid.*, 16.
13 *Ibid.*, 17-18.
14 *Ibid.*, 21.

performed a miracle. "Indeed, I came to doubt the practical application of the biblical ethic of *agape* love, since the application of love in Jesus' life seemed to presuppose the transcendence of natural limits," Burkholder concluded.[15] Besides, Jesus' life "was not representative of ordinary life."[16] He did not marry, so he didn't have family responsibilities, he did "not run anything," he did "not report to a board or to a constituency,"[17] and he died at an early age. All this meant

> that the ethic of Jesus, especially as set forth by the Sermon on the Mount and the 'hard sayings' which presupposed simple one-to-one situations, is not an historical social possibility, because the ethical situation is ambiguous, ambiguity being grounded in nature and compounded by history. Therefore, one must do the best possible, which unfortunately will necessitate compromise.[18]

Reality requires that the Christian must compromise. Within the real world of family, business, and social organizations *agape* as lived and taught by Jesus is not a realistic possibility. This conclusion is central to Burkholder's thought. For his Christology this means that we cannot realistically follow Jesus, who was and is divine, because we are limited by our humanity. Hence we are saved through Christ's death and resurrection in spite of, not because of, our deeds. We are saved by grace. For reasons such as this Burkholder finds himself identifying with contemporary evangelical theology.

It was this kind of historical realism, learned especially in the Far East, that Burkholder took with him to Princeton, and his dissertation evidences the same methodological approach. He is obviously a student of Ernst Troeltsch and H. Richard Niebuhr in that his ethics are premised upon a vigorous, realistic social analysis. He is first a sociologist. Indeed, he is one of the foremost sociologists of the Mennonite situation, for his sociology is not premised on a utopian "ought" but on a realistic "is." To be sure, a normative "social responsibility" does serve for him as a hermeneutical principle to read history but only to clarify the realities of the Mennonite dilemma, not to soften their glare.

Social responsibility as defined by Burkholder is identical to "the feel for justice." "Social responsibility" and "justice" may be used interchangeably, as long as justice is used in the dynamic sense of regard for the needs and rights of others. Justice is simply "the ability to see one's self and one's interest in the total social context with a view to the general welfare."[19] Social responsibility

15 *Ibid.*, 16.

16 *Ibid.*, 19.

17 *Ibid.*

18 *Ibid.*, 35-36.

19 *The Problem of Social Responsibility*, 197.

also means accountability for the world and identification with the world;[20] it "is really political responsibility broadly conceived,"[21] including the possibility of assuming political office.[22] In a reformulation of Troeltsch's "sect" and "church" types Burkholder suggests that:

> A church may be said to be socially responsible if it seeks to produce a Christian culture including the political order without necessarily stipulating how this is to be accomplished. On the other hand, a church which declines the task of Christianizing the total social order but prefers to concentrate on the church as a separate body and therefore refuses to enter into the problems of society as a whole, may be said to reject social responsibility.[23]

This second kind of church is obviously the same as Troeltsch's sect.

Burkholder's "Christianizing the social order" motif, or the notion of a "Christian culture," is from today's perspective of religious and cultural pluralism rather triumphalistic and even archaic. Further, his *a priori* identification of the church with social responsibility and the sect with social irresponsibility could suggest that, given his commitment to social responsibility, Burkholder is completely abandoning sectarianism. Fortunately, he quickly modified this apparently undialectical and uncritical approach to social responsibility. Indeed, his critique of the Mennonite ethic of the 1950s was precisely that it was not adequately dialectical. Mennonites assumed "the possibility of the unambiguous embodiment of an ethical ideal."[24] They needed to realize that their situation was not that simple. Rather the dialectic or dilemma is

> one of conflicting duties. Love itself demands responsible participation in society for it is in the social realm that the Christian meets the neighbour. To avoid responsibility is the same as 'passing by on the other side' unless it can be proved that the neighbor can be helped more effectively by some other way than through the legitimate channels of social action. Thus the contemporary Mennonite who is committed to the high ethic of Christ and who is on the other hand aware of the opportunities to meet human need through participation in the struggle for social justice is caught in a genuine dilemma.[25]

The essence of that dilemma is, Who is my neighbor?

Over thirty years later Burkholder still speaks in these dialectical categories.

20 *Ibid.*, 15.
21 *Ibid.*, 18.
22 *Ibid.*, 16.
23 *Ibid.*, 20.
24 *Ibid.*, 31.
25 *Ibid.*, 25.

This emphasis on the dialectical, on dilemma, on tension and paradox allows him, even requires him, to struggle with both the problems and the possibilities of the Mennonite community. He does not simply chastise Mennonites on the basis of an idealistic "ought," but seeks to understand why sociologically that ideal cannot be attained under modern conditions. He remains a sectarian, however chastened, as well as a realist.

As a sectarian realist Burkholder does not aim simply to convince Mennonites that they must become socially responsible, although this is surely a constant theme of his. Rather his primary agenda is to seek a balance between contemporary realities and a sectarian heritage. For him

> the question is whether American Mennonites, who are now increasingly caught in the "whirl" of American life, will be able to avoid at least some of the adverse experiences of other sects by the knowledge of the problem gained through modern social sciences. Will it be possible for at least one dissenting group of the Reformation to maintain some of the peculiar doctrines and practices of the faith in the modern period in the face of the seemingly relentless forces of conformity to the general practice of society?[26]

What was the Mennonite dilemma of the 1950s, according to Burkholder?

> It was the struggle between the traditional Mennonite 'way of life' and social involvement. The logic of Mennonite theology, ethics, and history points in the direction of radical rejection of social responsibility for the sake of a 'new and separated' people. However, the logic of present day social, economic and educational tendencies among Mennonites points towards greater involvement and responsible participation in the affairs of the world. Sociologists and historians who are familiar with sectarianism know that this problem is bound to appear sometime in the lives of all idealistic, separatistic communities.[27]

This problem is sometimes referred to as "routinizing the charisma," or the problem of the second generation. Jesus and his disciples, as well as early Anabaptism, were first generation, charismatic phenomena. Short of artificially forcing repetitive first generation revolutions as the Maoists attempted, institutionalization inevitably results in establishing structures to maintain and to translate the new to succeeding generations. A primary example is, for Burkholder, the family–an institution assumed by most Christians as necessary yet not particularly emphasized by either Jesus or the early Anabaptists. Yet such structures are, for Burkholder, of primary importance to society and culture: "to any group which continues to exist for any length of time, regardless of its cultural indifference, there comes a time when the permanent structures

26 *Ibid.*, 3.
27 *Ibid.*

of natural existence must be given their place."[28]

North American Mennonites, however, sought to avoid this reality. Even as they found themselves increasingly involved in business and industry, education and missions, rather then developing a theology of social responsibility, which would acknowledge their situation, they sought to maintain a first generation sectarianism. The primary vehicles for this were a recovery of the Anabaptist vision, a social ethic premised on nonresistance, and a withdrawal into "Mennonite community." While obviously finding value in each of these strategies Burkholder concluded that they were dysfunctional for modern Mennonites.

For Burkholder, as for most of the "recovery" champions, the Schleitheim Articles of 1527 typified Anabaptism.[29] He summarized his detailed analysis of Schleitheim Anabaptism thus: "The genius of the Anabaptists . . . was their pure biblicism, their total preoccupation with the idea of the Kingdom of God and therefore their complete neglect of the great problems of cultural life in the world."[30] For those Mennonites who sought to recover Anabaptism as normative for the twentieth century, the Schleitheim approach was not a problem because, says Burkholder:

> Mennonites have never recognized a tension between the command of Christ and the principles of natural social existence. They are opposed to the general stream of history but they still hold to the possibility of an unambiguous social order which will include all the natural elements of life. Mennonites have declared confidently that 'all' of life must be 'Christianized' and by 'Christianized' they mean that all can be brought into perfect harmony with the will of Christ.[31]

This Schleitheim perspective is naive, Burkholder contends. It has a "limited view of culture" which does not recognize "the unique problems of social organization."[32] Because "bureaucracy, impersonality and complexity make pure love only an occasional possibility," Mennonites preferred a simple agrarian lifestyle.[33] Yet this agrarian response to modern society is "romantic." It is also dangerous because it identifies one cultural form of the church with the Kingdom of God.[34] And with reference to the meaning of nonresistance:

28 *Ibid.*, 128.

29 This equation of Anabaptism with Schleitheim was surely unfortunate. Had Burkholder considered Pilgram Marpeck, for example, he would have found a form of Anabaptism more sympathetic to his own concerns.

30 *The Problem of Social Responsibility*, 86.

31 *Ibid.*, 131.

32 *Ibid.*, 133.

33 *Ibid.*, 134.

34 *Ibid.*, 152-153.

"Mennonites will do little or nothing to disturb the equilibrium of social and political forces providing they are given the privileges of living a quiet and godly life in isolation."[35] Their energies are focused upon "the unique problems of the preservation of the sect."[36] Even when Mennonites in the 1950s were addressing social problems through voluntary service, Burkholder concluded that "as a matter of principle, Mennonites congregate where *agape* may be expressed least ambiguously, i.e., where relations are simple, most direct and least political."[37]

As a realist, Burkholder argues that, a theology which is functional must square with reality. "Business organizations, educational institutions and even highly organized mutual aid societies cannot operate by the pure principles of the 'love feast'."[38] Mennonite Mutual Aid, Goshen College, and Mennonite businesses "at their best" operate with "an amalgam" of Christian virtues in combination with classical "natural" virtues. "Such are the ways of the world at their best," says Burkholder.[39] This is the way Christian organizations must function although, to be very sure, this is not the way of pure, selfless *agape*. Hence he concludes, as earlier noted, that

> the present crisis of Mennonite life will require a revision of the present Mennonite approach to society. Mennonites must realize that they are a part of the world system and that they share the guilt and responsibility for corporate evil and that their attempts to be obedient to Christ and 'be' the true church must take into consideration the 'ambiguities' of their actual situation. In the end only "this realistic approach will prevent perfectionistic illusions and despair."[40]

II

Burkholder need not have worried about "perfectionistic illusions and despair"–not that Mennonites in the last thirty years heeded his counsel and thus avoided the problem. Far from it. Rather they essentially redefined the dialectic in order to avoid despair.

Confronted by Burkholder's doctoral thesis, the church fathers of the day responded predictably. They suppressed his analysis by discouraging the official church press from publishing this heresy. And heresy it was, because it directly challenged the carefully nurtured strategy of Harold S. Bender, Guy F.

35 *Ibid.*, 175.
36 *Ibid.*, 175.
37 *Ibid.*, 182.
38 *Ibid.*, 223.
39 "Reflections," 49.
40 *The Problem of Social Responsibility*, 223, and "Reflections," 53.

Hershberger and others to maintain and to revitalize the unique and separatist identity of the Mennonite Church through a recovery of "the Anabaptist vision."

The next generation of Mennonite scholars, who essentially were in Burkholder's age cohort, for the most part followed the same strategy of suppression. Led by certain members of the so-called Concern group, their agenda was not a chastened but a radicalized sectarianism.[41] The ecclesiology of Bender *et al.* was considered by some of this group's spokespersons to be too compromised by denominationalism. Burkholder did not share their perspective. Of those students of Bender and Hershberger who parted company with their teachers, most moved in one direction, while Burkholder was one of the lone voices who moved in the other.

Sadly the voice of Burkholder, out of phase with the majority position of his contemporaries, virtually fell silent. After Burkholder joined the faculty of Harvard Divinity School, his voice was little heard in the reshaping of Mennonite thought. Among the many reasons was the message itself. An ethic of ambiguity and dialectics does not lend itself to ready pamphleteering, as does the "prophetically" idealistic admonition to follow the way of Jesus. Besides, college and seminary professors, the primary Mennonite ideologues, can live more comfortably in ivory tower idealism than fellow believers in business, the professions, and administration–with whom Burkholder identified because of his experience abroad. Then too, especially in the 1960s and 1970s, Mennonite college and seminary students, unencumbered by the realities of life, most not yet married, were ready to follow their professors in championing a radical sectarianism against their compromising elders. Although his commitment to political engagement and to a Christian embracing of justice and power should have endeared him to the new Mennonite activists of the 1960s and later, this was not to be. With reference to an earlier era he commented: "My inclinations were to refuse such simple either-or solutions to the problem as those of Bender, Hershberger, and Concern in the 1950s, when Schleitheim, the undisputed source of Mennonite ethics, pointed to a clean, consistent, and undivided ethic of withdrawal."[42] The following decades largely abandoned sectarian withdrawal but retained idealistic sectarian either-or solutions. Burkholder's emphasis upon ethical ambiguity surely muted his voice.

But not only was his perspective rarely heard until very recently. Burkholder argues that steps have been taken since 1958 to avoid the dilemmas he posed. What were these avoidance mechanisms? For one thing, particularly under the tutelage of John Howard Yoder, "irresponsibility" became a virtue. In *Concern* No.1 (1954) Yoder declared irresponsibility to be "an implication of the Mennonite view of the church" of which Mennonites ought not to be ashamed.

41 On the Concern group, see *The Conrad Grebel Review* 8.2 (Spring 1990).

42 "Reflections," 28.

Burkholder interprets this view to say: "Not to be responsible for the moral decision-making of society at large is an implication of discipleship and must be made a presupposition of Mennonite ecclesiology. Not to be responsible is not a matter of neglect rooted in a lack of social awareness but is rather a logical implication of the sectarian ethic."[43] To this Burkholder responded: "I could not disagree with the logic of sectarian ecclesiology, but I could not be happy with it."[44]

Similarly, and secondly, Mennonites were taught not to "feel responsible for the outcome of history." According to Burkholder, Yoder "declares that Christians should not feel responsible for the outcome of history. He reinforces his position by the obvious fact that you can never know how history will turn out."[45] Burkholder considers this position to be "unloving and uncaring. The outcome of history is the outcome of the neighbor; to love one's neighbor is to care for the neighbor's history."[46]

Thirdly, "Jesus is domesticated according to demand," says Burkholder. Because for Mennonites the teaching of Jesus "cannot be dysfunctional," Jesus is redefined so that he "must have meant what makes sense to us." In turn, "the Mennonite Church no longer insists upon discipleship in its radical form. The gate has been widened." Discipleship "now means 'solidarity' with Jesus, whatever that may mean concretely, rather then literally 'following after'." Much discipleship talk is "loose talk." Gone is an emphasis on sacrifice. Discipleship language now generally refers to something between the extraordinariness of Jesus' ethic and the everyday reasonableness of civil righteousness. Emphasis has shifted from observable concrete actions to motive, intention, and character.[47]

According to Burkholder, "perfectionism is patterned in the Gospels, it is not occasional or accidental." But more recently the perfectionism of Jesus has been transmuted to allow Jesus to remain normative in spite of all the acculturation that is characteristic of contemporary Mennonites. Says Burkholder: "discipleship and Christianity are becoming tautological, and that is serious for Mennonites in light of traditional claims." He objects to "sliding scale a discipleship," a process where discipleship is "redefined to reduce or remove the tension between the perfectionistic ideal and contemporary reality."[48]

Burkholder implies that a fourth mechanism is being utilized to simplify the dilemma, namely the reinterpretation of Anabaptism. He grants that our

43 *Ibid.*, 31.
44 *Ibid.*
45 *Ibid.*, 48.
46 *Ibid.*
47 *Ibid.*, 40-42.
48 *Ibid.*, 41.

understanding of Anabaptism today is much more complex then when he wrote his dissertation. Yet it is definitely not accurate to identify as Anabaptist every cause related to social action and social justice, as some contemporary Mennonites are wont to do. Justice is not an active category in the Anabaptist lexicon, and Burkholder is surely right to note that "historically, justice has not been accepted as a Christian category by Mennonites."[49]

Even the ambiguities of politics have been rendered harmless to avoid the dilemma. In Yoder's *Politics of Jesus,* political involvement has been redefined as prophesy. This work represents a major shift that Mennonites made during the 1960s. Yet, says Burkholder, "politics" in Yoder's book is a euphemism in the sense that politics, as the term is normally used, includes what Yoder rejects, namely "participation in the actual formulation of law, legislation and the enforcement thereof." In brief, "to speak is finally 'admissible,' but not to govern."[50]

What particularly disturbs Burkholder about this approach to politics is that it is so limited. While making a place for witness, Yoder "makes no place in the life of the followers of Christ for real, earthly kingship, or its modern democratic equivalent." Burkholder insists not only that power be included in any legitimate definition of politics but also that Christians should participate in real politics as well as in prophecy. Why? One goes into politics to serve the neighbor–"the neighbor being human beings who benefit through the ministry of just laws, humane structures, imaginative policies, and enlightened diplomacy." For example, although Mennonites have recently moved into "disinterested peace mediation," Burkholder maintains that often "the most effective peace processes are those which are carried out by participants in diplomatic services." Some of the greatest peacemakers in this century have been public servants, he adds.[51]

The second problem he sees with the prophecy school of Mennonite political involvement is its false notion of purity. Mennonites have generally assumed that they remain ethically unblemished as prophets, while others who serve as responsible lawmakers and administrators in the public realm are morally culpable. Responsibility is attached only to those who make decisions. But this is illusory. Burkholder wrote after the UN invasion of Iraq:

> The first casualty of Mennonite political witness is the myth of Mennonite purity, since we are involved in political reality. Even those who have little to say to the political order are deeply involved in the 'the political realm' . . . if we take it upon ourselves to exercise our democratic rights to counsel the government on anything from sewage disposal to Desert Storm, we will find

49 *Ibid.*, 37.
50 *Ibid.*, 43.
51 *Ibid.*, 43-46.

that we have entered a world of ambiguity and compromise. This is the dilemma faced by anyone who becomes involved in politics. But the political dilemma can no longer be avoided, apart from radical withdrawal from the social order.[52]

Yet again Mennonites frequently avoid this political dilemma. Ambiguity and loss of purity is not generally admitted, so long as governments are admonished to act according to the way of Jesus. This is particularly true for those who are proponents of what Burkholder describes as "universal christological nonviolence." For these Mennonites, because "nonviolence is an absolute principle based upon the message of Christ," governments must be told "that all policies presupposing violence must be abandoned."[53] Although governments will not and indeed cannot act upon this "prophetic" word short of allowing for anarchism, the prophets can feel confident in their faithfulness, not least because they have been faithfully "irresponsible." Burkholder asks,"What right has one to prophesy without accepting responsibility for decision-making, management, and accountability?"[54]

Burkholder identifies other mechanisms whereby Mennonites have avoided "perfectionistic illusions and despair." But these suffice to suggest how he reads what has happened in the Mennonite Church in the last thirty years. Obviously Mennonites have become much more involved in the world in recent decades. *War, Peace and Nonresistance* is no longer defining Mennonite ethics–in fact, it is hardly read any longer. But despite his earlier plea for Mennonites to become socially responsible, Burkholder is not overjoyed at what has happened. He would say, I think, that the trajectory of Mennonite thought has significantly compromised the life and teachings of Jesus, even though Mennonites have no room for compromise in their theology. By contrast, he retains an uncompromising understanding of the rigorous way of the Cross, even while arguing that Mennonites must allow for legitimate compromise within the relativities of history.

The reason for this difference is that Burkholder is fundamentally realistic, while most Mennonite theologizing remains essentially idealistic. He is a realist about sin: original sin, individual sin, "personal sins, willfully committed, but also social sins, structurally necessitated," the "subtleties of sin and the ambiguities of existence." He is a realist in knowing that, although saved by God's grace, he remans sinful. He owns for himself Luther's dictum *simul justus et peccator*. As a realist he is much more an evangelical then a liberal,

52 J. Lawrence Burkholder, "What Shall We Then Say To The State?" *Gospel Herald* (Dec. 31, 1991), 6-7.

53 J. Lawrence Burkholder, "Mennonites on the Way to Peace," *Gospel Herald* (Feb. 19, 1991), 3.

54 "Reflections," 47.

more Augustinian then Pelagian.[55] For Burkholder, the Anabaptist vision as defined by Harold S. Bender is inadequate as the basis for a Christian life that embraces social responsibility. Discipleship is not the essence of the gospel, only *of* the essence. Discipleship should temper Luther's emphasis on justification but not replace it. "The Anabaptist Vision refuses to acknowledge the tragic side of life from which the purest of saints and the greatest of moral adventurers need to be saved," Burkholder maintains. Hence "life in this world can be sustained only by God's forgiving grace"–as defined in the classical doctrines of justification by faith and the objective atonement.[56] "For while the doctrine of justification has been put to bad use as an excuse for sin," says Burkholder, "I feel called to draw upon its best articulation for good use since the Anabaptist-Mennonite concept of grace is inadequate." He concludes: "My moral sense, having been enlivened by the Anabaptist Vision, is kindly assuaged by a doctrine of grace as developed by Augustine and the Reformers."[57]

J. Lawrence Burkholder speaks as a Mennonite ethicist with refreshing candor and honesty. He articulates and embodies the stance of sectarian realism: a position needing to be heard in and beyond the Mennonite churches today as never before. He dare not be silenced once again! Undoubtedly attempts are being made to do just that, not least by resorting to the same domesticating mechanisms he repudiates.

55 *Ibid.*, 49-51.
56 *Ibid.*, 49.
57 *Ibid.*, 51.

The Socially Active Community: An Alternative Ecclesiology

J. Denny Weaver

I

J. Lawrence Burkholder's dissertation of 1958[1] issued an important challenge to Mennonites, namely to accept responsibility in the public, political arena. The following essay offers a reformulated definition of the believers church, and this new formulation becomes the foundation for the thesis that the issue of social responsibility is really a conversation about the nature of the church.

While Mennonites belong to the ecclesiological tradition known as the "believers church" or the "free church,"[2] ambiguity persists about the meaning of these terms. All would agree that the free church refers to separation of church and state and to the rejection of a state church. "Free church" poses a contrast to the "established church" that has characterized western Christendom for most of its history. The Anabaptist reformation of the sixteenth century eventually developed into the first instance of a free church in the modern era.[3] The term becomes ambiguous in North America, however. Since the church was officially disestablished two centuries ago, and separation of church and state constitutes a cardinal principle of national ideology, all North American churches are "free churches."

It would be generally agreed that "believers church" connotes the voluntary nature of Christian faith and commitment to the church. Baptism of adults marks that voluntary decision. This understanding is the alternative to the *Volkskirche*, the church that encompasses the entirety of a supposedly Christian society.

J. Denny Weaver is Professor of Religion at Bluffton College, Bluffton, Ohio.

1 J. Lawrence Burkholder, *The Problem of Social Responsibility from the Perspective of the Mennonite Church*, (Elkhart, Indiana: Institute of Mennonite Studies, 1989).

2 Franklin H. Littell, *The Origins of Sectarian Protestantism: A Study of the Anabaptist View of the Church* (New York: Macmillan, 1964); Donald F. Durnbaugh, *The Believers Church: The History and Character of Radical Protestantism* (New York: Macmillan, 1968); James Leo Garrett, Jr., ed., *The Concept of the Believers Church: Addresses from the 1967 Louisville Conference* (Scottdale, Pa.: Herald Press,1969).

3 Recent Anabaptist historiography has shown the social, evolutionary nature of this emergence, in contrast to the older historiography, which described rejection of the state church as a principled decision from the beginning. See Harold S. Bender, "Church and State in Mennonite History," MQR 13.2 (April 1939): 83-103; "The Anabaptist Vision," Church History 13.1 (Mar. 1944): 67-88; J. Denny Weaver, *Becoming Anabaptist: The Origin and Significance of Sixteenth-Century Anabaptism* (Scottdale, Pa.: Herald Press, 1987).

Since Christian nurture begins with birth into the *Volkskirche*, baptism of infants quite logically follows. However, the distinction between membership by birth or voluntary decision also breaks down in North America. With no established church, in a sense adherence to any church is voluntary, whatever its practice of baptism. Without explanations, all North American Christians could regard themselves as associated with "believers churches."

At the popular level, "believers church" lends itself to other distortions. If it is misunderstood to imply that people in other church traditions are uncommitted or are even unbelievers, the stress on believers can sound like a self-congratulatory claim to a superior churchly status. Emphasis on the voluntary nature of faith can easily be transformed into American individualism that overshadows the church as believing community. "In the believers church," I once heard a colleague say, "everyone gets to make up his own theology."

For these reasons, while "believers church" and "free church" have clear historical meanings, it is inadequate to identify the believers church in terms of voluntarism and separation of church and state. As preparation for responding to Burkholder's challenge to social responsibility, the following develops some additional dimensions of believers church ecclesiology, using series of three questions to focus these distinctions.[4]

II

Question one: Is the church (called to be) different from the world?

The immediate answer appears to be yes. Ultimately, however, the answer is based on christology. If Jesus is the normative revelation of the will of God, then the church with Christ as its head must by definition pose a contrast to the world that does not profess Christ.

When the question is posed in generalities, most Christians would agree that the church is called to be different from the world. But while the theological answer is indeed yes, the functional answer frequently becomes no. Assessing the question in terms of the so-called "Constantinian shift" shows that much of western Christendom has indeed affirmed that the church need not be different from the world.[5]

Constantine legalized the Christian religion with the Edict of Milan in 313

4 The following questions are not new. All appear in some form in the statement of the findings committee from the first conference on the concept of the believers church. Garrett, *The Concept of the Believers Church*, 314-21.

5 The following description of the Constantinian shift follows John Howard Yoder, "The Constantinian Sources of Western Social Ethics," in *The Priestly Kingdom: Social Ethics as Gospel* (Notre Dame, Ind.: University of Notre Dame, 1984), 135-47.

AD, adopted Christianity as his own religion, and began treating it as the official religion of the Roman empire. When Theodosius made the Nicene version of Christian faith the law of the empire in 381 AD,[6] the church encompassed all of the Roman empire. Profound changes in ecclesiology accompanied this shift from minority to majority status. The church became identified less as the people of God and defined more in terms of its hierarchy and its sacramental functions. Western society became the assumed bearer of God's providence. The welfare of the church was now linked to that of the empire–a threat to the empire implied a threat to the church, while a theological dispute could split the empire. The reference point or norm for public behavior and public accountability thus shifted from Jesus and the church to the emperor and what was good for the empire. The exigencies of political office became the arbiter of acceptable public behavior. The church now accepted killing in the name of the empire–war–as a necessary compromise for the sake of preserving Christian society. For ease of reference, this series of evolutionary changes has been given a sobriquet such as "Constantinian shift" or "Constantinian synthesis."[7]

The church of the Constantinian synthesis is not really different from the world. It accepts the world's–the empire's–public ethics and political outlook. Rather than witnessing to or posing an alternative to the social order, it supports the society and its institutions.[8]

Much of the modern Christian tradition stands within this Constantinian tradition. Much of western Christianity still perceives the western world as a society based on Christianity, and supports killing in the name of the state. North American society has a deep and abiding sense that politics defines social reality. Thus to confess that the church should be different from the world is a statement which has the potential to distinguish the believers church from much of North American Christianity.

III

Question two: (a) Is the product of God's grace saved individuals or a saved people? (b) Is the church a voluntary assembly of saved individuals, or is the church as a people intrinsic to the gospel?

6 R. P. C. Hanson, *The Search for the Christian Doctrine of God: The Arian Controversy 318-381* (Edinburgh: T. & T. Clark, 1988), 821, 849-56.

7 It should be emphasized that this series of changes happened gradually, and was well under way already in the mid-second century. Constantine is more the symbol than the agent of these evolutionary changes.

8 "The place of the church or of persons speaking for Christian morality (including academic theologians) is that of 'chaplaincy,' i.e., a part of the power structure itself." Yoder, *Priestly Kingdom*, 138.

These related questions deal with the inner reality and structuring of the church. Believers church ecclesiology stresses the voluntary nature of faith. Whether the church is a voluntary assembly of believing persons or an intrinsic part of the gospel, either answer assumes the voluntary nature of individual faith and thus justifies claims to be a believers church.[9] However, in spite of their parallel appropriation of the label "believers church," the two constitute quite different views of the church.

Understanding the church as a voluntary assembly of the saved means that God's saving activity primarily envisions individuals, or that the individual is the primary object of God's grace.[10] These saved individuals then gather for worship, mutual encouragement, and admonition. Thus it is the piety and spiritual experience of individuals that constitute the primary content of this version of the gathered, believers church.

In contrast, if the church itself belongs to the essence of salvation, then God's grace saves or transforms structures and relationships as well as individuals. While salvation clearly has a personal component, the salvation of individuals receives its fullest meaning and significance through the church–as a peoplehood. That is, salvation involves transformation of relationships among individuals and of an individual's relationship to God. Salvation includes social ethics.

Once again, attitudes towards violence can illustrate the difference between the church as the voluntary assembly of the saved and the church as intrinsic to

9 For example, see the seven characteristics of the believers' church identified in Durnbaugh, *The Believers' Church*, 32-33; and the five characteristics of the "free church syndrome" noted by John H. Yoder, "The Free Church Syndrome," in *Within the Perfection of Christ. Essays on Peace and the Nature of the Church*, ed. Terry L. Brensinger and E. Morris Sider (Nappanee, Ind.: Evangel Press and Brethren in Christ Historical Society, 1990), 171. These lists of characteristics can encompass either answer to the questions that head this section.

10 Thomas Finger suggests that the modern, western assumption of democratic principles makes it difficult to take the church seriously. When the foundation of government is defined in terms of John Locke's "social contract," by means of which government structure has authority "through voluntary common consent," modern people find it hard "to think of church structures, leaders, decisions, teachings, or ceremonies as having any intrinsic reality and authority." Thomas N. Finger, *Christian Theology: An Eschatological Approach,* vol. 2 (Scottdale, Pa.; Kitchener, Ont.: Herald Press, 1989), 226-28; citations, 228. Along these same lines, as a critique of the way Mennonites have considered the church, C. Norman Kraus wrote: ". . . we have tended to consider the church under the model of a democratic institution rather than as the 'body of Christ.' Put crassly, but with more than a grain of truth, we have viewed it as a nonprofit corporation formed by freely contracting individuals (its actual legal status under the United States Constitution) for their mutual purposes of nurture, inspiration (worship), and evangelism. From this perspective the church, however solemnly we speak of it, belongs to the *bene esse* and not the *esse* of salvation." "Toward a Theology for the Disciple Community," in *Kingdom, Cross and Community: Essays on Mennonite Themes in Honor of Guy F. Hershberger*, ed. John Richard Burkholder and Calvin Redekop (Scottdale, Pa.; Kitchener, Ont.: Herald Press, 1976), 111-12.

salvation. Since Jesus demonstrates that the reign of God rejects violence, the church which is intrinsic to the gospel and is testifying to the reign of God cannot discard pacifism without ceasing to be the church. This is not true if the church is a voluntary assembly of the saved. In this case, a resort to violence or the church's support of state violence is "merely" the failure of fallible human beings and does not fundamentally challenge the church's character or its ministry to the piety of individuals.

My analogy for understanding these two approaches uses athletic teams. Consider the very different relationships among members of track and football teams. The member of the track team is an autonomous individual. Her training is her own, and participation in a meet is her own, individual effort. The team is functionally secondary–a device for keeping score, a source of inspiration. But the team itself has no fundamental impact on an individual's participation or performance in a meet. Whether the high jumper knocks the bar off on her first three attempts has no effect on the miler's winning run.

Now consider a football team. While an individual may work out alone, he cannot play football without a team. It is the team which gives meaning to his individual workouts, as well as to his activity and expression of himself as a football player. And all players share in the performance of the others, whether a running back's fumble that leads to a loss or the kicker's last-second field goal that wins a game.

The entire biblical story pictures a people–God's people–as the primary entity through which God works and is revealed in the world. God called Abraham, and promised that his descendants should become a great nation in which all the nations of the earth would bless themselves. That is, the promise finds fulfillment in a people. That people was the children of Israel. They fell into captivity in Egypt; God rescued them. They occupied Palestine, followed by another exile; God rescued them again. The New Testament introduces Jesus as the most complete revelation of God. At the beginning of his ministry Jesus assembled followers, who were the nucleus of the people of God, a people of God in continuity with the old but constituted a new way. The church in the twentieth century is the continuation of that nucleus, whose roots go back to Abraham. It is an ineradicable biblical principle that the church exists as a product of God's grace, as an intrinsic component of the gospel.

Posing the question about the church as integral to the gospel has clear implications for one's evaluation of the Constantinian synthesis. The church as a voluntary assembly of sincere individual Christians can exist comfortably within the "Constantinian" church that denotes western society as nominally Christian. This kind of gathered community focuses on individual piety and ethics, while accepting the inherited established church social ethic which reflects or supports public and governmental exigencies. But when the church itself is integral to the gospel, social ethics different from the social order belongs to salvation. This church cannot comfortably co-exist as a subset of the

Constantinian church.

A particular manifestation of the church as the voluntary assembly of the saved corresponds to the cell groups of pietism, the movement that originated as an effort to add an experiential component to the mass church.[11] Within the mass church of Christendom the purposefully saved gathered voluntarily in small groups for mutual encouragement and admonition, but without claiming to have a social ethic for the entire church and without a sense that the voluntary assembly spoke in a universal way. While the early pietist movement had a strong social emphasis and pioneered in such things as humane treatment of the mentally ill, after the generation of Spener and Francke, pietism developed quite an individualistic cast.[12] This voluntary assembly continued to allow the state or mass church to represent universality, and thus to imply that society as a whole is the bearer or representative of God's providence.[13]

Discussion question two deals primarily with the inner reality and structuring of the church.[14] However, rejecting the equation of western society with the people of God, and affirming that the church belongs to the gospel in an integral way, makes acute the question of how Christians work in the world. The following section focuses on the relationship of the church to the wider society and the world.

IV

Question three: (a) Is Christian social responsibility expressed primarily through the church or through the institutions of society? (b) Does the church

11 C. Norman Kraus, *Community of the Spirit* (Grand Rapids: Eerdmans, 1974), 17-19.

12 Dale Brown, *Understanding Pietism* (Grand Rapids: Eerdmans, 1978), 35-37.

13 Finger's treatment of sanctification and ecclesiology acknowledges implicitly the two kinds of believers churches as well as the correspondence of pietism to the voluntary assembly of the saved. When Finger discusses personal sanctification, his primary believers church example is John Wesley, whose Methodist movement was a pietist reform within the Church of England. When he discusses believers' church ecclesiology, his primary example is Harold Bender's "Anabaptist Vision," which Finger calls "inherently corporate." Thomas Finger, *Christian Theology*, vol. 2, 204-207, 236-40. While Finger acknowledges that his own statement of ecclesiology corresponds most to the model of the believers churches (*Christian Theology*, vol. 2, 268), his overall methodology–to draw elements from all the models of ecclesiology he surveys–serves to make the believers church one of several inadequate ways to understand the church, rather than demonstrating that it is a viable, historical alternative to the various forms of Constantinian ecclesiology. At the same time, however, Finger's statement of his own ecclesiology would correspond to a believers church ecclesiology as I would understand it.

14 Whether the church is a voluntary assembly or a product of grace has implications for a number of other discussions for which space precludes treatment here. The list might include: the relationship of conversion, baptism, church membership; the meaning of worship, spirituality, church, ethics; the understanding of what constitutes religious and churchly activity, and of discipline and its scope.

permeate society, working through societal institutions as an invisible presence, or does it function as a visible alternative to the existing society and its institutions?

These questions raise the "Constantinian" issue in another form. Western Christendom has long assumed that the church permeates society. This assumption emerged in the aftermath of the Constantinian synthesis, when all people became de facto nominal Christians. Since the identity of true, that is, sincere, Christians could be known only by God, the true church came to be considered an invisible presence permeating society. Although North America has no established church, much of North American Protestantism and Catholicism continues to perceive the church in terms of the permeation model rather than as an alternative to the social order.

In the permeation model, the responsibility toward society which an individual Christian may feel receives expression primarily through the institutions of society, rather than through the church. Thus Christians and the church become, in effect, a support group and the conscience of the wider society. Further, when Christian social responsibility is expressed through the structures of society, its strategy and effectiveness get evaluated and measured according to societal criteria rather than criteria of the reign of God that Jesus embodied in his person.

In contrast, according to the historic Mennonite understanding, the church poses an alternative to society. This stance characterized the church prior to Constantine. Sixteenth-century Anabaptism constituted one of a number of more recent historical manifestations of that model.

How one understands the avenue for social expression has major implications for the program of the church, and the structures through which Christians express their social concerns. Some questions indicate the difference between the permeation model and the alternative society model. For example:

þ Do we foster peace by working through government to influence Jean Chrétien and Bill Clinton, or by working through MCC, Christian Peacemaker Teams, or Witness for Peace?

þ Do we help the homeless by getting elected to public office so that we can vote more money for public housing, or by working for Habitat for Humanity or for MCC in Appalachia?

þ Do we work at the problem of education for minorities–or for Mennonite students, for that matter–by getting elected to public office in order to shape governmental policy on education, or by becoming a development officer or a professor for a Mennonite college?

- þ Do we try to prevent crime by focusing on punishment and incarceration or by supporting Victim–Offender Reconciliation Programs?

The choice between government structures or church institutions for the primary expression of social concern provides an eloquent testimony to where we really believe that God is working in the world.

By this point, it should be quite clear that the question of social responsibility is not whether the church can or should be responsible. It obviously should. Rather the debate concerns the primary avenue for expression of that responsibility. Should it happen primarily through church-related structures or government institutions? For Christians, primary loyalty belongs to the church which is called to pose an alternative to the social order.

Distinguishing the avenue for social responsibility has clear implications for the future shape of Mennonite peace theology. Historic Mennonite peace theology began with the well-known, baseline position called "biblical nonresistance." Often the Schleitheim articles are claimed as the historical beginning point and model. For Mennonites, biblical nonresistance meant to face evil passively, offering no resistance of any kind. That position has come under the justifiable critique that such nonresistance does nothing to bring about justice or to correct evil situations. Instead of acquiescing passively, it is argued, heretofore passive Mennonites need to assert themselves actively, to "get involved," to "be relevant," to bring about justice.

A frequent assumption is that such relevant activism will require some level of involvement and compromise with the institutions and structures of modern society. The debate then concerns the tolerable level of involvement–how to retain enough nonresistance to be loyal to Mennonite tradition, while accepting enough compromise to attain some level of relevance. One can visualize this search as a continuum running from (irrelevant) nonresistance at one end to (relevant) violent involvement on the other end.[15]

This continuum assumes that Christian social responsibility happens primarily through societal and governmental structures as agents. It assumes that greatest effectiveness occurs through the eventual use of the government's means, namely violence and war, with the criteria for success and relevancy also supplied and defined by those structures. It is a neo-Constantinian outlook. It reflects Reinhold Niebuhr's analysis of nonresistance and social

15 This continuum approximates the church-sect typology first articulated by Ernst Troeltsch and since then passing through a series of refinements. See Ernst Troeltsch, *The Social Teaching of the Christian Churches*, I, trans. Olive Wyon (New York: Macmillan, 1931; New York: Harper Torchbook, 1960), 331-43; Benton Johnson, "On Church and Sect," *American Sociological Review* 28 (August 1963): 539-49.

responsibility.[16]

This continuum measures the church's increasing identity with the state and its becoming comfortable with governmental structures. However, it becomes evident that a single continuum cannot account for all possibilities. One can also visualize a continuum of social involvement through the church which retains the rejection of violence as the limiting norm of engagement. This second continuum also begins with biblical nonresistance, but it measures increasing confrontation between church and society. Maintaining the rejection of violence as a norm, it stresses the church as the agent of change and as a visible alternative to the existing social order.

On the second continuum, the lowest level of nonviolent confrontation between church and society could begin with legal means, such as petition of legislatures and use of the court system to seek redress. It might progress to public, but still legal, demonstrations and boycotts. A small step up might be a refusal to display symbols of patriotism or military support in time of war. Another increment might involve civil disobedience, and the deliberate breaking of laws deemed unjust or inappropriate. Examples include the lunch-counter sit-ins of the 1960s, and the various vigils and illegal enterings at nuclear plants. Another increment in intensity might include actions actually to impede or prohibit violence or injustice–such as the destruction of draft registration records or the use of human bodies to impede bulldozers or military machinery. In every case of confrontation, there would be the inviolable principle of refusing to use violence and do harm to people. Such refusal would appear in its starkest form when nonviolent participants refuse to retaliate against violence and continue to suffer nonviolently in the case where the particular nonviolent action should fail.[17]

If the first continuum describes social involvement increasingly in terms of societal and governmental structures, the second has an increasing focus on the distinction between church and society. The nature of alternatives and the degree of confrontation of unjust structures, however, depend more on the character of the wider society than on the church. The extent to which the nonviolent church finds itself at odds with its host society will differ greatly

16 See, for example, "Why the Christian Church is Not Pacifist," in *The Essential Reinhold Niebuhr: Selected Essays and Addresses*, ed. Robert McAfee Brown (New Haven: Yale, 1986), 102-119.

17 It is what happens after the failure of a particular action or movement that perhaps most distinguishes Christian nonviolent resistance from nonviolent resistance of another kind. In the midst of the particular involvement there may be no functional or tactical difference. When a nonviolent confrontation or action fails–and some most certainly will fail–a group which used nonviolent tactics on practical grounds might choose to abandon nonviolence on the same practical grounds. Christian nonviolence, for which Jesus' teaching and example are normative, would maintain its nonviolent stance in the face of that same failure, rather than abandon the norm of Jesus Christ.

among various cultures and countries. Frequently, the exercise of social responsibility through the church does not mutually exclude its exercise through societal structures. For example, church and nonchurch groups could cooperate in petitions to government or in use of the courts to seek redress on a justice question. The church and the social order might cooperate in activities concerning education, housing, or health care. One clear purpose of the church's social involvement is to engage the institutions of society and to seek to shape public policy.

However, visualizing the second continuum indicates that involvement in North American politics and North American violence is not the only path to social responsibility and relevance. The intersection of interests and the possibility of cooperative actions ought not to seduce the church into assuming that it has a common foundation with the social order. Although occasionally co-belligerents, they are not allies. The calling of the church is to be the church, to witness to the reality of the Reign of God in the world, not to help the social order be the state.

Whether Christian social responsibility is expressed through church or society is more than a question of ethics and peace theology. It concerns the nature of the church. One formulation has a neo-Constantinian outlook, the other assumes that the church poses an alternative to the world. Expressing social responsibility through the church is another dimension of the church that is intrinsic to the gospel rather than merely a voluntary assembly of saved individuals. It is another dimension of the church which is "called to be different from the world."

V

J. Lawrence Burkholder's challenge for Mennonites to accept social responsibility was in dialogue with another version of believers church ecclesiology. It differed in several respects from the model sketched above.

Burkholder's dissertation challenged a believers church model which I call the "withdrawn alternative community." This ecclesiological model claims roots in scripture[18] and in the sixteenth-century Anabaptism represented by the two-kingdom teaching of the Schleitheim Articles[19] and Harold S. Bender's "Anabaptist Vision."[20] As Burkholder pictures this Mennonite believers church model,[21] its goal is to create an alternative community that stands as an island of

18 Burkholder, *Problem*, 63.

19 *Ibid.*, 69.

20 *Ibid.*, 40.

21 While some might want to dispute Burkholder's reading of Schleitheim, "Anabaptist Vision," or Guy F. Hershberger, whom Burkholder cites as a prominent spokesman for the position he challenges, the present discussion focuses on Burkholder's perception of that ecclesiology, and

saved and just reality in the midst of the sinful world, to create separate but parallel structures to the world.[22] Jesus' absolutist, nonresistant ethic was indifferent to the socio-political order, and therefore does not apply to civilization and culture.[23] This alternative community defines Christianity as discipleship, which has the four dimensions of suffering, nonresistance, missions, and rejection of worldly culture.[24]

With reference to its inner workings, this alternative society touches all dimensions of life, both individual and corporate. Its foundational social principle is love, whose most basic form is absolute biblical nonresistance.[25] Love or nonresistance refuses absolutely to impose anything against the will of another, even in matters of good and evil. That refusal places not only war off limits, but also labor unions,[26] the holding of political office, and responsibility for justice in society,[27] each of which involves an element of coercion. As Burkholder described this withdrawn alternative society, it forces a choice between faithfulness to the gospel on the one hand and responsible action in the world on the other. Schleitheim and the traditional Mennonite community recognized the necessity of the state and the use of force by civil authorities for the sake of preserving public order. However, offices of the state and the state's exercise of force fall outside the perfection of Christ, and Christians do not participate in them.[28] Since rejection of the sword and the magistracy is a denial of politics as a Christian vocation, the stance is clearly a call for withdrawal from society,[29] and the responsibility for government and world order fall into the hands of unchristian people.[30]

Burkholder compared this vision of the withdrawn alternative community to the Corpus Christianum, which assumes responsibility for the world. As he describes it, the Corpus Christianum confesses Jesus as Lord of all reality, which means that the state belongs to the orders of creation. The Corpus Christianum thus assumes responsibility for all dimensions of human life, including the political, and the church assumes responsibility to guide the course of the world.[31] Since the Corpus Christianum recognizes the lordship of Christ over all of reality, including politics, it seeks unity, includes all persons

the significant points he wants to make about relevancy and responsibility.

22 Burkholder, *Problem*, 148f.

23 *Ibid.*, 27-28.

24 *Ibid.*, 38-87.

25 *Ibid.*, ch. 3; 53.

26 *Ibid.*, 151.

27 *Ibid.*, 133.

28 *Ibid.*, 68-70.

29 *Ibid.*, 72.

30 *Ibid.*, 116.

31 *Ibid.*, 96.

under its authority, and seeks to bring all people together rather than polarizing them into believers and unbelievers.[32] Whereas Anabaptism withdrew from the world in order to remain true to God (and thus was pure but socially irresponsible), the Corpus Christianum considered it a divine calling to organize basic human structures in the social and political realm (and was thus tainted but responsible).[33]

Burkholder does not advocate that Mennonites adopt the outlook of the Corpus Christianum, but he does offer several comments about the Mennonite alternative community on the basis of learnings from it. He believes that Mennonites cannot actually withdraw from the wider society and truly produce the pure alternative community.[34] Supposed neutrality and noninvolvement actually supports the dominant forces and the status quo.[35] In fact, he believes, Mennonites are already involved in the wider society in ways that include the enjoyment of technology, education, voting, some local office holding,[36] and vocations in business and the professions.[37] Through organized voluntary service Mennonites have attempted to express some social responsibility in ways unmixed with the nationalism and hatred of war.[38] Thus Mennonites have already compromised with society, Burkholder believes, and they would do well to consider how they might assume some responsibility for the society in which they are already participating and with which they are already compromised and compromising.

Further, Burkholder contends that the withdrawn alternative Mennonite community should acknowledge the lordship of Christ over all of creation rather than seeing Christ primarily as Lord of the church. Confessing Christ as Lord of all creation would move Mennonites to assume some responsibility for society as a whole as well as to accept responsibility for what happens within the church.

Burkholder is uncomfortable with the fact that the alternative community seems to leave the reins of government in unchristian hands. It would seem appropriate, he believes, for persons with Christian morality to serve in positions which have responsibility over all of society.

The wedge which the alternative community appears to drive between the Christian community and the unregenerate world also causes Burkholder discomfort. He considers the focus on the church and the withdrawal from

32 *Ibid.*, 97, 117.
33 *Ibid.*, 82.
34 *Ibid.*, 93, 197, 132.
35 *Ibid.*, 174-75.
36 *Ibid.*, 163-66.
37 *Ibid.*, ch. 3; 22.
38 *Ibid.*, 178-85.

political responsibility to be nearly a tacit denial of the lordship of Christ over all reality. While the free church does not repudiate the general idea of the penetration of all structures of corporate life by the Christian spirit,[39] it does mean that such wider contribution happens on a voluntary basis,[40] and that in practice little attention is given to the relationship of Christ and the gospel to society as a whole.[41] Whereas the Corpus Christianum aims to unify all of reality under the lordship of Christ, the alternative community polarizes church and world in the name of Christ.[42]

On the basis of this critique, Burkholder offers two specific suggestions. First, Mennonites should develop a rationale and a theology for the use of power. Eschewing power absolutely would mean removing Christians from the world. As a specific power compromise between nonresistance and the "compulsion and force" of the world, Burkholder calls for Mennonites to consider nonviolent resistance. It would approximate the absolute ideal of nonresistant love while affording an opportunity to participate in the ambiguous struggles for justice in society.[43] Second, he calls for Mennonites to develop a concept of justice. That is, they should develop an emphasis on the world's social problems in addition to the nearly exclusive focus on the church. With their past focus on love rather than justice, Mennonites have shown a tendency "to shy away from the social problems of the world where justice, rather than pure love, characterizes both the method and the goal of social action."[44]

In no way does Burkholder consider these suggestions to be an abandonment of traditional Mennonite values. Rather, he argues, Mennonites will continue to pursue "the traditional goals of brotherhood, peace and mutuality," but with a difference. Rather than focusing on a pure church based on absolute obedience, using the compromise of nonviolent resistance will compel Mennonites to "take into consideration the 'ambiguities' of their actual situation."[45]

VI

In several later publications, Burkholder carried further some themes from his dissertation. A series of lectures delivered in 1960 developed the ideas of love and justice. In his definition, love applies primarily to relationships among

39 *Ibid.*, 106, 114-17, 214.
40 *Ibid.*, 106.
41 *Ibid.*, 214.
42 *Ibid.*, 114-17.
43 *Ibid.*, 223.
44 *Ibid.*
45 *Ibid.*

individuals whereas justice describes the way an organization deals with people. At the level of individual relationships, love is unlimited. In contrast, at the level of institutions, where justice defines behavior, the particular needs of each individual cannot always be met in caring for the need of the whole. There is thus an inherent tension, Burkholder believes, between love and justice. He offered three suggestions for making institutions as sensitive as possible to love: "attention must be focused on the most needy"; "organizations and institutions [should] take a flexible attitude toward policy"; "accept people within the terms of their own individuality."[46] This contrast between individual and institutional relationships develops further his belief that responsible activity requires compromise.

In a 1976 essay, Burkholder developed a more complete comparison of nonresistance and nonviolent resistance, and issued a vigorous appeal in favor of nonviolent resistance.[47] On the one hand, he contrasted nonresistance and nonviolent resistance. They exhibit profound differences and exist in inherent tension with each other. Whereas nonresistance absolutizes the freedom of others, nonviolent resistance accepts aggressive confrontation which places constraint on others. On the other hand, advancing beyond his dissertation, Burkholder described a very significant point of agreement between nonresistance and nonviolent resistance. They have the same foundation, "namely, the life and teachings of Christ."[48] Since Jesus confronted the rulers of Israel through such acts as healing on the Sabbath and criticizing the Pharisees, Burkholder argued that Mennonites should adopt nonviolent confrontation as an acceptable way to work at issues of justice in the wider society. The point is that the choice is not between nonviolence and nonresistance "but between violence and various forms of nonviolence." Christians should consider "both nonviolent resistance and nonresistance [as] genuine alternatives to violence; they belong together in the same life."[49]

While he anchored nonviolent resistance in the life and teaching of Jesus, Burkholder nonetheless considered it a compromise with the purity of nonresistance. "It would behoove us, however, to seek an ethic which stops short of violence but which at the same time makes a place for the necessities of

46 J. Lawrence Burkholder, "Love and Justice in Mennonite Mutual Aid," in *The Compassionate Community: A Collection of Lectures Presented at Conferences of the Association of Mennonite Aid Societies*, ed. H. Ralph Hernley (Scottdale, Pa.: Association of Mennonite Aid Societies, 1970), 51-77; quotes, 71, 73, 75.

47 J. Lawrence Burkholder, "Nonresistance, Nonviolent Resistance, and Power," in *Kingdom, Cross and Community: Essays on Mennonite Themes in Honor of Guy F. Hershberger*, ed. John Richard Burkholder and Calvin Redekop (Scottdale, Pa.: Herald Press, 1976), 131-37.

48 *Ibid.*, 134.

49 *Ibid.*, 135.

personal and corporate existence."[50] His language echoes the influence of Reinhold Niebuhr when Burkholder suggests that the practice of nonviolent resistance involves "conditions of compromise," the acceptance of "ambiguities" and sharing in "the guilt and responsibility for corporate evil."[51] Rhetorical questions posed by Burkholder show that he feels such compromises would pose a danger to Mennonite peace practices and pacifism as they begin to move along the continuum toward violence. Nonetheless, it is a danger they must face, he believes, and it belongs to the ambiguity of the modern world. Facing that situation, Burkholder concludes, calls "for creative imagination, [and] courage to face suffering."[52]

These comments on nonviolent resistance indicate both Burkholder's commitment to the nonviolence of Jesus and his belief that nonviolent resistance was a necessary compromise for the sake of justice. Burkholder's language for nonviolence places him on the first continuum discussed earlier, in which nonviolence occupies a middle position between irrelevant nonresistance and relevant violence, rather than on the second, which considers rejection of violence a norm and measures degrees of confrontation with society.

In his most recent statement on nonresistance and nonviolent resistance, Burkholder seemed to treat several Mennonite approaches to nonresistance and nonviolence in another way.[53] He described pacifism as a "wide–ranging cluster of logical and reinforcing ideas," and sketched four differing stances found among contemporary Mennonites. They include "traditional 'biblical' nonresistance," three varieties of "witnessing nonviolence," "dialectical pacifist political responsibility," and "vocational pacifism." Rather than arranging these on a continuum, Burkholder appeared to grant them all equal validity as options within the Mennonite church. He suggested that the "plethora of modifications" be interpreted "as a sign of vitality"[54] for a Mennonite commitment to peace theology.

Burkholder's remarks on the church since his dissertation reveal a certain ambivalence about the nature of the church. On the one hand, as he noted in the

50 *Ibid.*, 137.

51 Burkholder, *Problem*, 223.

52 Burkholder, "Nonresistance, Nonviolent Resistance," 137. In a 1988 essay, Burkholder stated: "A peace theology would frankly face the dilemmas of pacifism but would insist that in the 'interim' between the advent of Christ and the consummation, compromises, of which there are many, would stop at the point of killing human beings. For to kill a human being is to remove him or her from the realm of repentance, renewal, and salvation." "How Do We Do Peace Theology?" in *Essays on Peace Theology and Witness, Occasional Papers No. 12*, ed. Willard M. Swartley (Elkhart, Ind.: Institute of Mennonite Studies, 1988), 33.

53 "Mennonites on the Way to Peace," *Gospel Herald*, 19 Feb 1991: 1-4, 8.

54 Burkholder, "Mennonites on the Way," 8.

conclusion to the dissertation, he retains much from the traditional Mennonite view that the free or believers church should pose an alternative to the world. In 1972 he described his vision for a new, urban Mennonite community. It would provide intentional community, likely meet in homes, allow freedom and individuality among members, and engage in political action. At the same time, it will "seek to perpetuate what is best in the Mennonite tradition without apology," and while engaging in cooperation with other Christian bodies "will affirm the tradition and seek to incorporate as many of its values as possible." While engaging in political action, their small base will mean that the main thrust of Mennonites "cannot be to influence the social and political structures." Instead, it will be to form a community which will enable people to relate to others in depth, to find forgiveness, reconciliation, comfort, and encouragement as well as an intellectual understanding of Christianity. The Mennonite community will be the community from which one gets perspective by which to live and work in the world as servants and witnesses for Jesus Christ. It will help provide roots into the past and an eschatological reference for the future, both of which are sorely needed to combat the anonymity, confusion, and hopelessness of modern life.[55] When read in light of the discussion question of section II above, such comments can still be interpreted as an affirmation of a traditional yet revisionist view of the church that poses an alternative to the world.

At other points, Burkholder appears to modify believers church ecclesiology in the direction of the established church tradition. Alongside free church motifs, established church motifs become visible when his ecclesiology is analyzed in relation to distinctions made in sections III and IV above. In 1968 he suggested that the believers church should appropriate the social gospel's sense of social salvation and the authentic Christian existence of pietism. This combination would bring the salvation of the individual and the social order into one conceptual framework. When Burkholder describes where these motifs are being actualized, one sees the potential modification of the believers church model. Acknowledging that few believers churches embody this vision fully, he calls it "one of the exciting facts of our time that many ideas and practices which have been emphasized by the believers church are being introduced piecemeal into the established churches–Protestant and Catholic." He concludes by asking rhetorically: whether future developments will render outmoded the distinctions between church, sect, and established church; whether the Catholic church might find ways to join believers church fellowship to its massive, authoritative institution; and "Whether the future of the believers church lies in the local congregation or in the *ecclesiola in*

55 "Evangelism–the New Mennonite Community," *Gospel Herald* 65.40 (10 Oct 1972): 816-17; and "The New Mennonite Community," *Mennonite Life* 27.4 (Dec 1972): 104-05.

ecclesia."[56]

At this point, I take some exception to Burkholder's view. Wedding the authenticity of individual Christian existence from the believers church to the social order of the established church is not really the expansion or actualization of the believers church. It is rather to adopt the orienting framework of the Constantinian or established church that permeates society. This church allows the social structures to define the parameters within which Christians work. This approach is not really a new form of the believers church but is rather the way established church advocates understand that the church will gradually through permeation transform all of society under the lordship of Christ.

From the standpoint of practice, in Burkholder's view, the church often functions as an aggregate of individuals in the expression of social responsibility. He noted that individuals and the church express it differently. The church, for example, is less likely to take an active role in politics than is the individual. The church as an organization under the conditions of democracy usually hesitates to take a stand on political issues unless there is a rather clearly defined moral or religious question involved. Usually the church does not associate itself with a particular political party, though this has on rare occasions happened. But the individual Christian expresses his liberty by party affiliation and membership in competitive associations without violating principle. While social responsibility ordinarily refers to the attitude and action of individual Christians, it is possible to speak of socially responsible churches if meaning those denominations which make a place for responsible action by their individual members, whether they are kings, nobles, or magistrates of Reformation times, or presidents and statesmen of more recent times.[57]

However Burkholder might develop the theological statement of the church as intrinsic to the gospel, in the area of social responsibility his view of the church tends to see it functioning as a collection of saved individuals that permeates society, rather than as the community that poses an alternative to it. The operative assumption seems to be that the exercise of Christian social responsibility occurs when individual Christians become involved in various governmental structures. The more involvement in the political structures, the

56 "A People in Community–Contemporary Relevance," *Mennonite Life*, Jan 1968: 5-12. Even as Burkholder acknowledges that Mennonites have correctly rejected the Corpus Christianum, a similar willingness to accept the parameters of the so-called established church when dealing with providence and with social responsibility appears in Burkholder's "A query," *Gospel Herald* 80.43 (27 Oct 1987): 752-53. In another article, "What shall We Say to the State?" *Gospel Herald*, 31 Dec 1991: 5-7, Burkholder accepts violence by the state while saying that Mennonites should not participate in it, a position in agreement with Schleithem. At the same time, this article rejects Schleitheim's absolute separation, and suggests that Mennonites should become involved in the ambiguity of exercising social responsibility.

57 Burkholder, *Problem*, 20; see also 202-03.

more social responsibility is exercised and expressed.

It is on the subject of whether Christian social responsibility is expressed through the church or the institutions of society that Burkholder's ecclesiology has the most neo-Constantinian elements. As noted earlier, he located nonviolence on the continuum of involvement going from irrelevant nonresistance to responsible violence. That is already the way the established church would understand the problem. Further, Burkholder expressed two additional assumptions in line with the established church. First, he followed the Corpus Christianum in assuming that the ultimate expression of responsibility is in the public, political arena.[58] Second, along with the Corpus Christianum, he assumed that the full expression of social responsibility requires the exercise of force and violence.[59] In encouraging Mennonites to become socially involved, the discussion is by definition one of compromise–how much political involvement and how much force can and should they use without abandoning entirely their tradition of nonresistance? Posing the question this way uses parameters recognized and defined by the established church.

Burkholder has properly challenged Mennonites to move away from the model of a withdrawn church, and instead to accept some measure of responsibility for the course of society. While this move involves compromise and ambiguity, and a certain danger to the identity of the church, it is necessary, he believes. Nonviolent resistance constitutes his pre-eminent example of an acceptable compromise position; it begins with Jesus and keeps biblical nonresistance in mind while nonetheless allowing some form of engagement on behalf of justice in the world. Burkholder's view means some abandonment of believers church ecclesiology and the acceptance of some dimensions of established church ecclesiology. I understand Burkholder to be calling for some degree of compromise between the two. He envisions two basic options for Mennonite believers church social involvement—either withdrawal into Mennonite community or a compromised involvement along lines drawn by the established church.

VII

Burkholder posed the problem of social responsibility primarily in terms of a bipolar debate. His answer develops as some form of compromise or oscillation between the two poles. While I affirm his commitment to Christian social responsibility, I want to pose an alternative way of defining the issue. I suggest that the problem of social responsibility is not adequately defined in terms of a bipolar debate with options located along a single continuum. Rather than

58 *Ibid.*, 20, 26, 202-03.
59 *Ibid.*, 75, 174-75.

bipolar, it is actually a three-cornered debate, with a third option over against both the Corpus Christianum and the withdrawn alternative community. The three positions can be visualized in terms of a triangle, with each position in dialogue with the other two.[60]

At one vertex is the withdrawn alternative community with which Burkholder was in debate. Located at a second vertex is the church of the Corpus Christianum. At the third vertex stands the socially active alternative community.[61] Each stance is in dialogue simultaneously with the other two.

The Withdrawn Alternative Community. The withdrawn alternative community defines its primary identity in terms of obedience to Christ, and understands the church as the way to institutionalize that obedience. In spite of its stance, the withdrawn alternative community agrees with the Corpus Christianum on a number of points. They agree that Jesus taught absolute nonresistance as the Christian way, and that force is necessary in order to govern and rule the world. They part company on whether Christians should exercise that force. The withdrawn alternative community rejects the use of force absolutely, while the Corpus Christianum considers it a tragic necessity that belongs to its God-ordained duty to preserve the social order. The two positions also concur in seeing the problem of social responsibility as a bipolar question–one must choose either to obey the ideal of nonresistance or to compromise nonresistance for the sake of order in the world. Thus both agree that social responsibility is expressed primarily through the institutions of society.

From the bipolar outlook of the withdrawn alternative community, the socially active alternative community is another version–like the Corpus Christianum–of trying to run the world with compromised, less-than-Christ-like means. While the nonviolent resistance of the activist alternative community may be less evil than lethal violence, from the perspective of absolute nonresistance, nonviolent resistance is still clearly resistance. It is thus viewed as a compromise and a step along the continuum from biblical nonresistance to engaged violence.

The withdrawn alternative community accepts the status quo defended by the Corpus Christianum. Functionally this community therefore treats Christ as Lord of the church, with the sinful world located outside the perfection of Christ. While the withdrawn community may proclaim the gospel to all people,

60 This use of a triangle is stimulated by John H. Yoder's triangular depiction of sixteenth-century reformation options among Anabaptists spiritualists and magisterial reformers. Yoder, "A People in the World: Theological Interpretation," in Garrett, *Concept of the Believers' Church*, 254-57.

61 With 'alternative community', I intend to preserve the idea that the church is to be different from the world. The the designations 'socially active' and 'withdrawn' then indicate two stances toward the world.

the intent of this proclamation is not to transform the world, but to call people out of the world and into the church that is obedient to Christ and withdraws from the compromising practices of the world.

The Corpus Christianum. The Corpus Christianum agrees with the withdrawn alternative community on the absolutist character of Jesus' teaching about nonresistance, and also on the duty of the Corpus to exercise social responsibility by the use of force. Given its bipolar approach to social responsibility and its assumption about the necessity of force and violence, the Corpus Christianum regards the activist alternative community in much the same light as it does the withdrawn alternative community. It considers both nonresistance and nonviolent resistance as idealistic, absolutist, and unrealistic appproaches to justice and order in society. The Corpus Christianum is identified with and is a defender of the status quo, a point which mirrors the withdrawn alternative community's passive acceptance of the status quo. The church within the Corpus Christianum proclaims the gospel in order to transform individuals, who will then permeate the society and make its institutions more just. Thus, from a functional perspective, the Corpus Christianum treats the church as a collection of individuals.

Although the means and the terms would vary, the Corpus Christianum would agree on at least two general principles with the activist alternative community: that Jesus is Lord of all of creation, and that it is a responsibility of Christians to seek justice in the world. But it would disagree on the means for expressing those agreements.

The Socially Active Alternative Community. The activist alternative community agrees with the withdrawn alternative community that the church is different from the world, that its ethics is founded in the life and teaching of Jesus, and that rejection of violence belongs ineradicably to the gospel of Christ. The activist community agrees with the Corpus Christianum that Jesus is Lord of all creation, that Christians should have a concern for justice, that ethics has a social component. These two disagree both on the norm and the means for expressing social concern and social ethics. Whereas the Corpus Christianum expresses social concerns primarily through structures of government and uses criteria of effectiveness derived from the social order, the socially active community expresses these concerns through institutions of the church and claims Jesus as the norm for its ethics, whether individual or social. The activist community believes that the Corpus Christianum has removed Jesus from its social ethics, and supports Burkholder's view that the withdrawn alternative community has an inadequate social ethic and fails to address important issues and to seek justice in the world.

Only the socially active alternative community fully recognizes that there are three options. Only it can give full expression to the second continuum, which envisions degrees of resistance and confrontation while maintaining the rejection of violence as a limiting norm. Both the withdrawn alternative community and the Corpus Christianum see only a bipolar option and positions along one continuum, from nonresistance to violence.[62]

The activist community would agree with the withdrawn community that the church is intrinsic to the gospel. But the activist alternative community has a social agenda and a mission to promote justice in the world. It views nonviolent resistance as an appropriate and acceptable means to promote justice, whereas the withdrawn community considers that resistance as a compromise with violence.[63] This analysis shows why the nonviolent resistance advocated by Burkholder can be both accepted and rejected by people who profess Jesus' nonviolent norm–on one continuum nonviolent resistance is a compromise position along the path to violence, while on the other it is the limiting norm for the social involvement of the church in the world.

Unlike the other options, the socially active alternative community may challenge the status quo. The activist community proclaims the gospel both to call people into the church (in agreement with the withdrawn alternative community) but also to transform the society, with the socially active alternative community functioning as the agent of change.

In no way is this discussion to be construed as though the stance of the activist alternative community can solve all the problems of the church in the modern world. Burkholder's frequent allusions to ambiguity, dilemma, and paradox are relevant and must be taken to heart. I am suggesting, however, an alternative to his parameters for dealing with the ambiguity. I would argue that the proper Christian frame of reference for dealing with ambiguity in the social order is in terms of the continuum between the withdrawn and socially active alternative communities, rather than the continuum from the withdrawn alternative community to the Corpus Christianum. One can be genuinely unsure which of the available options expresses the least violent and most just course of action,

62 I suggest that it is this bipolar outlook of the withdrawn alternative community that accounts for the earlier Mennonite failure to accept Burkholder's argument for nonviolent resistance when his dissertation first appeared (See *Problem*, iv.). When viewed in light of the single continuum, nonviolent resistance appears as a compromise and a way station on the road to the acceptance of violence. When nonviolence is understood in terms of a third option, as the way the discipleship church involves itself in the world, nonviolent resistance has a positive connotation and it no longer feels like the first step toward abandonment of opposition to violence.

63 It could be argued that the term ""nonviolent resistance" unnecessarily carries negative connotations and stresses a mode of opposition rather than a goal toward which one is working. In that context, I would suggest the term "redemptive confrontation" as a possible designation for the way the socially active alternative community pursues justice in the world. On the other hand, given the profound faith in violence exhibited by North American society, I think it useful to keep before us the explicit rejection of violence, and thus have retained the language of nonviolent resistance throughout this essay.

but without assuming that that ambiguity leads to acceptance of some level of violence.

In the last couple of decades, a good many Mennonites have undergone a shift from passive nonresistance to acceptance of active nonviolent resistance. Burkholder's dissertation and the activities depicted in his autobiographical piece belong to the early, cutting edge of this shift, which is both valid and necessary. My concern is not so much to justify the shift, although the remarks above perform some of that function. My fear for the future of Mennonite peace theology is that peacemaking will be separated from the church. My intent is to develop peace theology and believers church ecclesiology such that the foundation of the shift remains anchored in ecclesiology; and to orient that shift from the withdrawn alternative community to the socially active alternative community.

It is important that nonviolent resistance not be understood as a compromise position located on a continuum stretching from nonresistance to violence. When the goal of social justice is viewed that way, movement along the continuum in the direction of violence seems inevitable. Always appealing to the same good intention, each compromise with violence lays the foundation for the next. Eventually the church has simply adopted the causes as well as the means and institutions of society at large.

Nonviolent resistance should rather be understood as the limiting norm of the church's involvement in the world. There are, to be sure, degrees of confrontation and involvement in the world on behalf of justice, but they are located along a continuum stretching from the withdrawn alternative community to the socially active alternative community. The difference between believers church and Corpus Christianum should not be the matter of social involvement but rather the method by which the church is involved, and the fact that Christians express their concern primarily through the church rather than through institutions of society and state. Thus nonviolent resistance is not a compromise halfway between pure but irrelevant nonresistance and impure but relevant violence. It is the way the faithful church is involved in the world.

In spite of the term 'alternative' used throughout this essay, the activist alternative community does not depend on 'over againstness' as a definition of the church. The church is not by definition in opposition to the surrounding society. The task of the church is to reflect and testify to the reign of God. The character of the surrounding society determines the extent to which the church finds itself in a state of being 'over against' the milieu. The difference in ethos between the United States and Canada provides one, easily accessible example. The United States has a monolithic, national civil religion, whereas Canada lacks such a civil religion. In contrast, Canada features a national cultural mosaic, in which differing religious and ethnic groups are expected and allowed to retain their individual character, whereas in the United States individual cultures are expected to lose their identity in a national melting pot. Thus, the activist alternative community has a greater sense of standing over against in the United States, where the national civil religion poses a powerful attraction for ultimate loyalty, than in Canada, where a national religious identity does not pose the same kind of national alternative to the church's identity.[64]

When the church–the activist alternative community–carries out its mission of being the church, some of its interests may overlap or intersect with the interests of other structures, including civil government and the state. Further, not every Christian can nor should work only in a church agency. At the point where interests of church and society correspond, it is quite appropriate for this community to cooperate with other structures. Such interests might include, but would certainly not be limited to, shelter for the homeless, hunger, education, health care, or the justice system. When engaged in that cooperative activity, however, members of the activist alternative community should remember that it is Jesus Christ through the church that shapes how they carry out the activity in a public institution. Both society at large as well as the members of the socially active alternative community have a common interest, for example, in educating people so that society can continue to function properly. However, Christians in the public school system should carry out that educational task on the basis of principles shaped by the church. Thus teachers might develop some alternative lesson plans, which include an alternative view of United States history, one that does not link freedom and violence. In times of national violence, such as the Gulf War of 1991, the socially active alternative community should be prepared to support its people within the public educational system who may experience discomfort because of the content of their teaching or their refusals to participate in patriotic acts in support of the war.[65] One could expand greatly the list of examples of how we can engage the institutions of our society through vocations shaped by a foundation in the activist alternative community.[66]

While the activist community may find itself engaging in cooperative activity

64 For a brief statement of these differences and their significance, see Harry Huebner and J. Denny Weaver, "We Dare Not Restructure Along National Boundaries" *Gospel Herald*, 22 October 1991: 8-10, and "Don't Stop at the Border," *The Mennonite* 106.20 (22 Oct 1991): 468-69. For a longer discussion, see Mark A. Noll, "The End of Canadian History?" *First Things*, No. 22 (April 1992): 29-36.

65 I am thinking for example of a teacher friend, who spoke of her great discomfort in the teachers' lounge during the Gulf War, when her classroom was the only one in the school without an American flag in the window as a symbol of support for the war.

66 On the basis of excerpts from an earlier draft of this essay, Duane Friesen posed questions about two possible readings of my language about social responsibility expressed through church or societal institutions. As a part of that conversation, I agree fully with his statement: "I believe we should both be the church and work in church institutions, and engage the institutions of society through our vocations and seek to shape public policy." Duane Friesen, review of *Mennonite Peace Theology:A Panorama of Types*, ed. John Richard Burkholder and Barbara Nelson Gingerich, in *The Conrad Grebel Review* 10.3 (Fall 1992): 349, n.2.

where its interests intersect those of the wider society, it must avoid the temptation of assuming that the intersection of interests implies a common foundation at a deeper level. The church has an identity that transcends any national identity and transcends identity with any particular cultural, ethnic, or geographic group. The church as church cannot become a nation or identify with a particular ethnic or geographic population—the Constantinian temptation—without losing its identity as a people of faith. It is thus inappropriate for the church to take on civil government as its own mission, even though at the point where their interests intersect, the church can and should offer advice to the government on issues of common interest or issues of justice and humanitarian concern.

The main thrust of this essay has been to show that the problem of social responsibility does not depend on a bipolar solution, where Christians committed to nonviolence must choose between either irrelevant and withdrawn moral purity or relevant but compromised activity in the world. A third option exists, namely the socially active alternative community, which proclaims the gospel with universal intent and which can intervene in the world on the side of justice using the means exemplified by Jesus. The position of such a community is socially irresponsible only if it is assumed that responsibility is primarily expressed through governments and that exercise of responsibility ultimately depends on violence. The essay has not drawn the blueprint for particular kinds of nonviolent social involvement and responsibility, but it has demonstrated that an ecclesiological foundation–a believers church foundation–does exist on which to formulate a comprehensive nonviolent approach to social responsibility.

Towards a Theocentric Christology: Christ in the World

A. James Reimer

Yoder, Kaufman, and Burkholder

John Howard Yoder, Gordon Kaufman, and J. Lawrence Burkholder are three contemporaries, all influenced by the Bender historical and theological renaissance of Anabaptist idealism, yet each finding a very different way of attempting to bridge Anabaptist-Mennonite idealism and modernity. Yoder's *The Christian Witness to the State* (1964), Kaufman's *The Context of Decision* (1961) and Burkholder's *The Problem of Social Responsibility from the Perspective of the Mennonite Church* (completed as a doctoral thesis in 1958, but not published until 1989), all conceived and written more or less during the same period, offer distinctive paradigms about how Mennonites ought to relate to modern culture.

Yoder's theology in *The Christian Witness to the State* is essentially a contemporary hermeneutic of Schleitheim, in which the church and the larger society/culture/state represent a dualism of response to the Christian message of nonviolence: "We need to distinguish between the ethics of discipleship which are laid upon every Christian believer by virtue of his very confession of faith, and an ethic of justice within the limits of relative prudence and self-preservation, which is all one can ask of the larger society."[1] The dualism between the church (made up of those "inside the perfection of Christ," and governed by nonresistance as laid out in Romans 12:9-21) and the world (made up of those "outside the perfection of Christ" and governed by the violence of the state as outlined in Romans 13:4), are both "ways of God's acting in the world." These are not two different realms but two different responses to God's way in Christ: one of obedience and the other of disobedience and sin. There is no place for compromise on the part of the Christian in his or her relation to society. The only options for Christians are to witness to individuals in the world in the hope that they will be converted to the perfection of Christ (*agape*, or self-sacrificial love) or to use "middle axioms" (the "pagan" language of justice, liberty, equality, fraternity, democracy, human rights) to communicate to the world in the hope that the world's behavior can be raised to a higher level. But

A. James Reimer is Associate Professor of Religious Studies and Director of Graduate Studies in Theology at Conrad Grebel College, Waterloo, Ontario.

1 John H. Yoder, *The Christian Witness to the State* (Newton, Kansas: Faith and Life Press, 1964), 23.

in no sense can the Christian enter the world of political compromise. It appears that Yoder has remained largely consistent in drawing out the logical implications of the schema articulated in this early work.

Kaufman, on the other hand, no longer accepts the strict dualism of response between church and world that characterizes Yoder's thought. Unlike Yoder's, Kaufman's theological position has evolved and changed substantially over the years. He explicitly states in later works that he was earlier much more ready to use the language of authority and revelation when talking about God and Christ. So when we look at his early book, *The Context of Decision*, we must remember that it no longer adequately represents his present thought. Having said this, however, it is still interesting to look at how even then his thought was quite different from Yoder's and contains hints of later themes. Kaufman, like Yoder, starts with the Anabaptism à la Bender view that "the radical sayings of Jesus set before us a clear picture of the ethical import of God's act, and that here is portrayed precisely the kind of conduct required in our relations with our fellows."[2] A christocentrism, understood as God's self-disclosure as self-giving love, is central to Kaufman at this point, as it is consistently for Yoder.

But for Kaufman this love penetrates human history and human society in general through the community of reconciliation. He continues to talk about a separation of church and world in this early work, and characterizes the empirical church as a "believers' church" along sectarian lines, yet he already clearly feels uncomfortable with the strict response-dualism of Yoder's Schleitheim. The community cannot afford to separate itself from the world if it takes its missionary task seriously. The church, seen both eschatologically and empirically, "is taking up the world into herself and transforming it into the community of the love of God."[3]

This rich image of the church taking the world into herself in the process of transforming the world has important ethical implications. The world is no longer seen simply in terms of apostasy (although Kaufman 'too' occasionally uses the term "rebelliousness" for the world) but as the place of human need, and the church no longer is a place devoid of sin but is made up of those living by the gracious forgivness of God. A 1958 *Concern* essay, published the same year Burkholder completed his doctoral thesis, shows what Kaufman's theological position means for ethics. "Love," he says, "goes to the very heart of the most sinful situations that it can find."[4] Love does not retreat from the realm of power

2 Gordon D. Kaufman, "The Church and the World," in *Nonresistance and Responsibility and Other Mennonite Essays* (Newton, Kansas: Faith and Life Press, 1979), 47-48. This essay is a reprint from *The Context of Decision* (New York: Abingdon Press, 1964).

3 *Ibid.*, 53.

4 Kaufman, "Nonresistance and Respnsibility," in *Nonresistance and Reponsibility*, 65. This essay was originally published in *Concern*, No. 6. A Pamphlet Series for Questions of Christian Renewal (Scottdale, Pa: Herald Press, 1958).

struggles, self–centredness, selfish individualism, domination, and exploitation, as Mennonites have historically tended to do, but enters into the heart of darkness in an attempt to transform it and bring it to light. Ethically this means that we also enter the political realm in the attempt "to help the society come to a deeper understanding of *its own* deepest convictions before God."[5] This may mean on occasion supporting a military bill which corresponds to the best insights of American society, and participation in the making of political policies with which we as individuals or a Mennonite community may disagree but which accords with the best insights of our nation. In a quotation that sounds remarkably like what Burkholder might say, Kaufman says:

> Yoder has argued for the recognition of a dualistic principle in Christian ethics which takes seriously the dichotomy between church and world, Christian and non-Christian action. The present essay has tried to take seriously the existence of this dichotomy, but without drawing the conclusion that this implies that the church need not 'assume responsibility for the moral structure of non-Christian society.' Rather, as God's agent here on earth—the very body of Christ—the church has absolute responsibility for the moral structure and activity of all of the world.[6]

It is this theme of the Christian's "responsibility for the moral structure and activity of the world" which preoccupies Burkholder's thought. It could be argued that Burkholder's paradigm stands midway between the position of Yoder and early Kaufman. He agrees with both that the starting point for Christian theological and ethical reflection and for moral action are the tough sayings and nonviolent love of Jesus. But Burkholder differs in how this is made concrete. He is as strong as Kaufman in his call for Christians to enter responsibly into the ambiguities of social and political existence. Where he differs, in my opinion, is that he has a keener sense of the inescapable contradictions, paradoxes, guilt, sin as wrongdoing, and tragedy of such social involvement. He is much more pessimistic and has a more tragic sense of life, a sensibility shaped by personal experience of suffering and death on the front lines of social action. There is less of the liberal and more of the neo-orthodox in Burkholder. This is perhaps expressed in the Conclusion of his 1958 doctoral dissertation:

> It is the writer's conviction that the present crisis in Mennonite life will require a revision of the present Mennonite approach to society. This is not to suggest that Mennonites should consider 'selling out' to world culture

5 *Ibid.*, 71.
6 *Ibid.*, 78.

> because of the intrinsic difficulties of embodying the ethic of Christ in the power arena. Rather it is to suggest that Mennonites must seek their traditional goals of brotherhood, peace and mutuality under the conditions of compromise. Mennonites must realize that they are a part of the world system, and that they share the guilt and responsibility for corporate evil, and that their attempts to be obedient to Christ and 'be' the true church must take into consideration the 'ambiguities' of their actual situation. This realistic approach will prevent perfectionist illusions and despair.[7]

Mennonites, according to Burkholder, will need to make a place in their theology for the ambiguities of the exercise of power, which in reality they already do in business life, educational institions, mutual aid societies, etc. They will need to give up the idea of nonresistance, which if followed literally would take them out of this world, and replace it with "nonviolent resistance." As well, they will need to find a place in their theological and ethical vocabulary for justice and the ambiguous struggle for justice. All this, without giving up the unique nonconformist witness of Mennonites to the world.

It is my view that Burkholder's theological and ethical paradigm ought to be compared with the other theological paradigms of his contemporaries, like Yoder and Kaufman, in order to help us understand his distinctive sociological analysis of Mennonite life and modern culture. I have just begun to think in these comparative terms, suggesting above a few lines of thought. In what follows I concentrate on Burkholder's own autobiographical reflections, bringing in some additional observations emerging from wider reading of his works, and I conclude with my own theological proposals concerning the direction I think Mennonites should be heading.

J. Lawrence Burkholder: Taking Responsibility for the World

The role of experience in theology

Where does Burkholder begin methologically? Christology obviously plays a central role in his theological ethic but experience, for him, is methodologically almost as important. One of the striking features of Burkholder's moving self-portrait as he gives it to us in his autobiographical essay,[8] is how concrete personal experiences shaped or modified his theology. His Mennonite upbringing and the influence of educators Daniel Kaufman, Harold Bender, and

7 J. Lawrence Burkholder, *The Problem of Social Responsibility from the Perspective of the Mennonite Church* (Elkhart, Ind.: Institute of Mennonite Studies, 1989), 223.

8 J. Lawrence Burkholder, "The Limits of Perfection: Autobiographical Reflections," in this volume.

Guy F. Hershberger firmly implanted in him the idealism of Jesus' love ethic as central to the gospel and a nonconformist/separatist stance toward the world. The memory of his mother's kindness to battered women in the 1930s reinforced his idealistic conviction that unselfish acts of Christ-like love were in fact possible. His studies at the Lutheran Seminary in Gettysburg introduced him to grace and to liberal pacifism as a politically prudential possibility—an optimistic attitude shattered by Hitler and World War II. His witnessing before the draft board on behalf of conscientious objectors brought him face to face with a Christian board chairman who asked some tough but intelligent questions which his background had not adequately prepared him for. His MCC relief work in India, his work as National Director of Church World Service in China and as Director of the National Clearing Committee of the United Nations in China, all led him in a new theological direction, quite distinct from that of Bender, Hershberger, and the Concern group.

What does it mean to take background, experience, and context seriously as theologically significant? It means that the human condition, the existential situation, the fact of sin, and life's ambiguities are taken into consideration in formulating one's theology and ethics. Here I stand with Tillich, when he argues for a method of correlation between the existential question and the theological answer. These experiential and social factors are not irrelevant to how one understands the very essence of the gospel. Further, it means recognizing as legitimate a diversity of views even on the most serious of topics, because people come from different backgrounds, and have different experiences of life. I teach a course at the Toronto School of Theology entitled "War and Peace in Christian Theology." I have Catholics, Anglicans, Evangelicals, Methodists, Presbyterians, Pentecostals, and occasionally Mennonites in this course. These different groups think differently about war and peace, depending on how they have been raised and what they have experienced. Many of them think very seriously about the issues and come up with different answers than I am used to as a Mennonite. To call them apostate because they reach different conclusions does not take seriously their experience, Christian faith and commitment, and struggle for moral integrity.

Burkholder's Christology: a Jesus of the Sermon on the Mount

It is fair to say that Burkholder's christology, except for a few wrinkles, stands firmly in the Mennonite tradition of the Bender, Hershberger, and Concern group. That is, the life and teachings of Jesus, as most clearly articulated in the Sermon on the Mount, are the basic point of reference for ethics. The Jesus ideal for discipleship is pure love, disinterested love, unreciprocating love, sacrificial love, nonviolent love, nonresistant love, *agape*–all terms Burkholder uses frequently and interchangeably. "I cannot escape the 'extraordinary'. . .

character of Jesus' demands," he says. "Perfectionism is patterned in the gospels; it is not occasional or accidental."[9] He is not about to weaken or soften the hard sayings and tough demands of Jesus in order to make life in this world easier. "We cannot avoid the 'offense' of Jesus' radicality .... Hence we must decide what to do with an 'impossible' ethic or, as Reinhold Niebuhr put it more positively, an 'impossible possibility'."[10]

This is why Burkholder is so critical of much of the contemporary middle class Mennonite talk of discipleship, what he calls a domestication of Jesus according to the demands of assimilation. Mennonites are now doing pretty well what everyone else is doing, without clearly admitting that a fundamental paradigm shift has occurred. "I am becoming slightly uncomfortable with the frequency and the unguarded use of terms like 'discipleship' and 'Anabaptism' when used to describe Mennonite middle class life in a democratic context of religious freedom such as ours."[11] He calls this "loose talk," which no longer means "the gold standard of Jesus' sayings as rigorous, sacrificial, 'upside down,' extraordinary, impractical Sermon on the Mount presuppositions."[12] Burkholder continues to hold that "all human relationships must be judged by their approximation to *agape*."[13]

Where then is the rub? What in his theology would make his thesis "inadmissible" to old and young Mennonites of the 1950s, and prevent it from being published? One word: "compromise."

Burkholder's ethic: love, justice and power

What made Burkholder's thesis inadmissible was not his christology *per se* but his claim that it was impossible historically to actualize and be obedient to the Sermon on the Mount ethic of Jesus, because every historical situation is morally ambiguous. As such it necessitates making compromises. One can realize the absolute ideal of pure love only proximately. Here Burkholder in fact has taken the Niebuhrian turn. It is in the world of ambiguity, complexity, and social responsibility that love meets justice (he defines justice as "love divided, distributed") and power (power is what is required to bring about justice). Mennonites, according to Burkholder, have never adequately come to terms with these two elements of all human life: justice and power.

Burkholder's autobiographical sketch is a moving account of how his personal experiences in India and China put on him the awful burden and guilt

9 *Ibid.*, 40.
10 *Ibid.*, 42.
11 *Ibid.*, 42.
12 *Ibid.*, 41.
13 *Ibid.*, 9.

that come with positions of power and social responsibility: when corporate responsibilities sometimes take priority over personal relations; when the language of rights, due process, and legalities takes precedence over consideration of particular human needs; when the need to fire a dishonest employee no longer justifies infinite forgiveness; when coercive measures need to be taken to evict refugees from an overcrowded evacuation plane; when military escort is requred to ensure safety.

Burkholder is the most persuasive in his analysis, in my opinion, when he moves away from the dramatic. His own personal experience in foreign service is certainly interesting and explains his own tragic dilemmas and problems with the historical impossibility of a pure love ethic. But for most of us they are not in the realm of our personal experience, and for that very reason they do not become a convincing critique of the historical Mennonite position. Also, his tendency to concentrate on the ambiguities of high-level government and politics tends to polarize positions before the issues are sufficiently clarified. Much more persuasive are his close-to-home examples, where we all live and have our being: marriage, family, institutional life of various kinds, life insurance, medicare, security benefits, business, wealth, education, art, music, and so on. It is on this level that we have *de facto* always made choices that compromise the radical Jesus ethic. Burkholder not only calls us to a new ethic of responsibility but to honesty in admitting what in effect always has been the case. We have always exercised power, for instance, in the church and in our educational institutions, and we ought to do so openly.

A theological proposal: a theocentric christology

Burkholder straddles two worlds: that of a traditional Mennonite sectarian ethic based on an Anabaptist Vision reading of the New Testament, and that of modern culture and its social demands. He finds himself firmly rooted in both and faced with the impossibility of living in both comfortably. He does not resolve this dilemma. While he is obviously attracted to the Niebuhrian option, he is less ready than Niebuhr to relegate one to the realm of the ideal and the other to the real: the two stand in more immediate tension with each other for Burkholder than they do for Niebuhr.

The question is, How do we as Mennonites now move forward into the future theologically and ethically? Where do we go from here? This is where I think Burkholder does not give us a great deal of help, although he offers some hints. I would suggest that in our attempt to find a viable moral and ethical stance toward culture we need theologically as Mennonites to go back to the drawing board in four areas: (1) our reading of the Bible; (2) our reading of church history, particularly early church history; (3) our reading of the sixteenth century Anabaptist movement(s); and (4) our reading of modern and post-modern culture.

(1) Our reading of the Bible

The church I belong to has a "Statement of Faith" that begins as follows: "To follow Christ daily in life, I will try to think, talk and act in the spirit that moved his acts and teachings. I must aim to do this day in and day out, in family, vocational, and social life. I recognize the Sermon on the Mount as Christ's guide for the Christian life." Here we have a pristine Bender version of what we as Mennonites are called to do. But is it adequate? A person from a Christian Reformed background who recently joined our church commented to me privately how inadequate she found this statement. And as I reflected on it I realized how narrowly we tend to define the basis for our ethic. The Sermon on the Mount in itself can simply not bear the freight that it is asked to bear. It does not give sufficient advice for family, vocational, and social life. We need the whole Bible as a guide for Christian life—a theology of the whole Bible, beginning with what I would like to call a theocentric christology.

A theocentric christology is one which (a) places the Jesus of the Sermon on the Mount within the context of the whole incarnation of the eternal Christ–the birth, life, teaching, ministry, death, resurrection, ascension of Jesus–and understands this Christ event in relation to (b) the God (Yahweh) of the Jews, as that God acted in Jewish history, and to (c) the Holy Spirit that gives birth to the Christian church and is present to the ongoing Christian community and to the world as God's continuing self-revelation. There is both a plenitudinous diversity within the biblical narrative and a comprehensiveness about the creation-fall/redemption-consummation drama that cannot be summed up exhaustively by the Sermon on the Mount ethic. To take the whole Bible as a guide for Christian faith would not mean that we treat all parts of it the same way but that we struggle with the Torah, Historical Books, the Prophets, the Wisdom Literature, the Gospels, the Acts of the Apostles, the Letters, the Pastoral Epistles, and the Apocalypse with equal seriousness.

I believe that the Sermon on the Mount ethic can and ought to continue to be the central ethical marker for Mennonites, but I doubt whether it ought to act as a canon within a canon. The Sermon on the Mount should itself be understood in the light of the whole Bible and not the other way around. To make it into a hermeneutical key with which to understand everything–the whole Bible, the whole of God's relation to the world–is to make ethics the starting point for theology. It is not clear to me where Burkholder stands on this issue, although I heard him say that, while discipleship is certainly important, Christian faith should begin and end with grace rather than with discipleship. I could not agree more.

The one wrinkle in Burkholder's christology that I mentioned above, which in my view gives it a different tone from the Bender-Hershberger-Concern Sermon on the Mount christology, is his attraction to the universal *logos* christology of Colossians and Ephesians. This brings a universal cosmic element into christology itself which transcends the more narrowly defined, literal Sermon on the Mount ethic, at least as normally understood by Mennonites. Also at various other points Burkholder strains at the Mennonite bit. He observes, for example, that Jesus' life was not representative of ordinary life: he never married, did not need to worry about looking after a family, did not run anything, did not pay taxes, had miracles at his disposal, was a free-lance, lived to be only thirty-three, and so on.[14] At another place Burkholder says he is drawn both to the radical discipleship rigor of sectarianism and the "'fullness' of Catholicity in which, quite apart from Constantinianism, an attempt is made to bring Christ to bear upon 'all things' essential to human existence."[15] But in the end he remains suspended between these two extremes, and thus ironically remains himself the dualist, a position which he criticizes in others. We need, in my opinion, as Mennonites to move forward theologically to a new synthesis, not as a way of escaping the tensions but as a way of offering viable witness to the modern world. I think we could do worse than to re-examine the early period of the Church and its attempt to come to terms with a fast-changing world in order to find some guidance for our own project.

(2) Our reading of early church history

I have argued strenuously that Mennonites need a trinitarian theology as a framework for their ethics, and have recently tried to show how the classical trinitarian orthodoxy of the early church both grows naturally out of the biblical materials and should be distinguished from the Constantinianism that Mennonites, together with other so–called "believers' churches," rightly reject.[16] Rather than concentrating here on trinitarianism, I would like to reflect briefly on what has come to be known as Constantinianism, because our view of this phenomenon has colored our whole attitude toward culture and politics.

It is for Mennonites almost a truism to say that Constantine and what he represents in the fourth century constitutes the fall of the church. I have shown in some detail, in the work noted above, how two interpreters of Mennonite theology, John Howard Yoder and J. Denny Weaver, are fairly representative of the Mennonite position on this question. Constantinianism embodies everything that is bad and apostate about the church. I would like to re-open the case, not necessarily to reverse the judgment.

14 *Ibid.*, 19

15 *Ibid.*, 30

16 A. James Reimer, "Trinitarian Orthodoxy, Constantinianism, and Theology from a Radical Protestant Perspective," *Faith to Creed: Ecumenical Perspectives on the Affirmation of the Apostolic Faith in the Fourth Century*. Ed. S. Mark Heim (Grand Rapids: Eerdmans, 1991), 129-161.

I want to propose that we have considered the third, fourth, and subsequent centuries too monolithically as the fall of the church, and written them off simply as the church accommodating itself to the state. This is a highly complex period, but here I will make just two observations about these early centuries.

The development within early Christianity that led to the so-called Constantinian synthesis was a direct consequence of the obedience to and success of the great commission of Matt. 28: 18-20: "All authority in heaven and on earth has been given to me. Go therefore and make disciples of all nations, baptizing them in the name of the Father and the Son and of the Holy Spirit, teaching them to observe all that I have commanded you; and lo, I am with you always, to the close of the age." This was a universal message, not a sectarian one. It was not a mandate to call the nations out of the world but to make disciples of them. We define discipleship too narrowly if we see it only in terms of nonconformist morality and ethics. Discipleship included spiritual regeneration and salvation. It was the seriousness with which the early church took these words of commission and its success that got it into trouble. The world, including high culture and politics, was drawn into the church.

In *Christianizing the Roman Empire A. D. 100-400*, Ramsay MacMullen explores why the non-Christian world was attracted to and came over to the church, and how authentic that coming over was.[17] He estimates that from the end of the first century there were in the order of half a million converts in each generation, that by 312 AD there were some 5,000,000 converts and by the end of the fourth century there were up to 30,000,000. With the massive influx of new members, particularly in the fourth century, the level of commitment to "discipleship" decreased, as people joined for mixed or nonreligious reasons. This is the dilemma for all missionary-minded movements like the early church, sixteenth-century Anabaptists, and modern evangelicalism.

There was considerable diversity in the type of solutions offered to the Christianity-culture dilemma in the period leading up to and during the fourth and fifth centuries. Tertullian (160-220 AD), living in passionate eschatological expectation, rejected outrightly Roman politics and society, and for the most part called for Christians to live in rigid, ascetic isolation from Roman culture, including not only the holding of office and military service, but also some forms of commerce, attending circuses, certain types of greetings, and so on. And yet, even he, anticipating the Mennonite Dordrecht Confession, believes the emperor serves a limited function in keeping the peace, restraining the evildoers, and protecting innocent people in the secular realm. To the extent that the emperor does this he should be obeyed.[18]

17 Ramsey MacMullen, *Christianizing the Roman Empire A.D. 100-400* (New Haven: Yale University Press, 1984).

18 Elizabeth Allo Isichei, *Political Thinking and Social Experience: Some Christian Interpretations of the Roman Empire from Tertullian to Salvian* (Christchurch, New Zealand: University of

Eusebius of Caesarea (c. 260-340 AD) represents the other extreme solution. He was a close friend and confidant to Constantine, a respected and influential churchman. He reluctantly supported the Nicene formulation of 325, was at the council (Tyre) that condemned the staunch defender of orthodoxy, Athanasius, and played a leading role in the council that readmitted Arius. Eusebius espoused a conservative political theology of culture, in which piety and temporal success are correlated. Constantine's reign was seen as the realization of the messianic age. Eusebius regarded Constantine himself as a saint, even the incarnation or vice-regent of the divine *logos*. The Christian Empire is the earthly image of the eternal archetype or exemplar in heaven. On the whole, western Christianity rejected this kind of fusion of theology and politics in favor of Augustine's solution.[19]

A contemporary of Eusebius was Lactantius. Somewhat paradoxical and inconsistent in his thinking, he was much more critical than Eusebius of the Roman empire, which Lactantius saw as the product of corrupted power and selfishness. Like Tertullian, in some of his earlier works at least, he was suspicious of wealth, condemned military service, war, plays and circuses, and warned against music and poetry. Only within the Christian community, within a dissident minority group, can God's golden age be restored. He called for social justice and economic levelling. Yet he rejected a Tertullian-like withdrawal, and tried to reconcile Christian theology with Greek philosophy and literature. As the attitudes of the Empire change toward Christianity he too became more conciliatory, and ended his life as a high-ranking employee of Constantine.[20]

It is Augustine (354-430 AD), however, who provides western Christianity with its classic solution to the Christian dilemma concerning Christ and culture. He is no longer able to see Rome as the eternal city and the crumbling empire as the actualization of the Kingdom of God. Like Tertullian, Augustine sharply distinguishes between Jerusalem (the city of God) and Babylon (the temporal city, the Roman empire or any empire), the first defined by love of God and the second by love of self and coercive power. But, unlike Tertullian, he does not counsel rejection and separation from the earthly city, which he considers a transient good. All states and empires, including the Roman, are for him fleeting realities. That which lasts is personal and spiritual attachment to Christ and God.

Augustine therefore both counsels inward detachment from the temporal city and supports the dutiful carrying out of societal tasks, including military service and government office. Because one's personal destiny far outweighs any other considerations, however, he subordinates the state to the church, and is willing

Canterbury, 1964), 27-40.

19 *Ibid.*, 41-57.

20 *Ibid.*, 58-71.

with some misgivings to recommend the use of force not only against those who invade the empire but against Donatist Christians themselves. This theocratic assumption, in which the church tells the state what to do, becomes the predominant theme of the Middle Ages.[21]

Our final example is Salvian, writing in the mid-fifth century, after Carthage had been sacked in 439 and after the decline of the empire was virtually complete. He no longer defends the virtues of the empire but, like the Hebrew prophets, denounces its sins, attributing its fall to the just punishment of a wrathful God for class division, official corruption, exploitation of the poor, imposition ofheavy taxation on the peasantry, and social injustice generally. He holds before society the absolute ideal of Christian monasticism, and somewhat naively reverses earlier contempt for the barbarians by idealizing them despite their theological Arianism. He is deeply pessimistic about strong political leadership, and calls for moral and spiritual regeneration.[22]

The point of these examples is that we ought not to demonize a whole era with one grand generalization: the Constantinianization of the Church. There was a rich diversity of attempts to come to terms with the changing fortunes of Christianity and its role within larger culture, some less acceptable than others. To call the whole period apostate is not to take seriously the struggle of the church, both its leaders and its members generally. Some of our theologians have tended to identify the theological development of trinitarian and christological orthodoxy with the so-called Constantinianization of the church. This is too simplistic an analysis of what happened, and does not take into acount the diversity of the period. That something went seriously wrong at the point where the church made the choice to theocratically identify itself with, and engage the state in, coercive suppression of dissent, heterodoxy, and diversity generally must not be covered up. To re-examine this period is not to soften our critique of what happened but to look empathetically at an age to see what we can learn from it in our own attempts to address similar dilemmas. To simply close the chapter on the fourth century, labelling it apostate, and thereby also to close the chapter on all other traditions—Catholic, Anglican, mainline Protestant—identifying them as heirs of that tradition, while identifying ourselves with the true church, is a form of self-righteous hypocrisy. We too are heirs of that tradition, we too face similar challenges in our relation to larger culture, we too make compromises. There never has been a pure church within history, a pristine Christian community.

21 *Ibid.*, 72-89.
22 *Ibid.*, 98-108.

(3) Our reading of Anabaptist history

Historian Werner Packull has recently put in serious doubt whether sixteenth-century Anabaptists actually lived up to the Anabaptist vision.[23] The twentieth-century Anabaptist ideal does not fit the sixteenth-century reality:"Revelations of bickering, of nasty interpersonal and group relationships–not to mention sexual failings and financial embezzlement among first-generation leaders–seem hardly the right stuff to inspire contemporary church renewal or stave off the inroads of secularization."[24] Early Hutterite leaders and their wives enjoyed special privileges at the table (good wines and better foods) in separate dining rooms not enjoyed by ordinary believers. They were authoritarian in their approach to leadership. Caspar Schwenkfeld, with some justification, accused Anabaptists of splintering into numerous sects for ridiculous reasons–"The Swiss, Hutterites, Gabrielites, Pilgramites, Netherlanders, Friesians, Mennonites, Hoffmanites, etc., ..."[25] Each tended to have self-appointed leaders accusing the other of holding to private property, despising proper leadership, disregarding family and economic obligations, sexual misconduct, and so on. In the end, Packull asks: "Could Mennonites, after all, learn something from the Augustinian tradition and Lutheran theology in regards to imperfection within the church, just as Lutherans should learn something from the Anabaptists concerning discipleship and separation from the powers that be?"[26]

It seems to me that ordinary Christians in our congregations have always recognized the reality of sin more clearly than the theological idealists, who develop ideologies of perfection. There is a dark underside to the Mennonite psyche which the official keepers of the tradition (preachers, deacons, patriarchs, theologians, teachers, bishops, ministers, leaders) have frequently managed to disguise through ingeniously contrived public personas, rules, regulations, myths, dogmas, and so on. The recent spate of abuse stories in our Mennonite media is making us all too aware of our imperfections right within the church. Myths about ourselves are being shaken regularly. Our artists and our journalists have frequently done a better job of communicating to us our true reality than have our theologians.

Burkholder has in his own powerful way struggled precisely with this contradiction between the Anabaptist ideal and the real world of sin, ambiguity, and moral dilemmas in which we find ourselves. He too, like Packull, in the end

23 Werner Packull, "Between Paradigms: Anabaptist Studies at the Crossroads," *The Conrad Grebel Review* 8.1 (Winter 1990): 1-22.

24 *Ibid.*, 21.

25 *Ibid.*, 15.

26 *Ibid.*, 21.

turns to the doctrine of justification and grace as a way of coping with this incongruity between the ideal and the real. The theological way forward for us as Mennonites in modern culture, I would argue, lies in two directions: a re-reading of Anbaptist history, which recognizes the diversity of possible connecting points beside Schleitheim; and a re-examining of other than Anabaptist theological traditions which can supplement and complement our own theological strengths.

(4) Our reading of modern and post–modern culture

Classical Christianity is under massive attack these days. This attack is coming from three major directions: (a) from those concerned with saving our planet who want a more environmentally friendly God; (b) from those concerned with social and economic justice who want a more historically active God; (c) from those concerned with dialogue between Christians and between religions who want a more ecumenical God. It is interesting to consider how each of these either complements or contradicts the other. All, however, have negative things to say about classical Christianity, whose God they see as too masculine and environmentally unfriendly, as too authoritarian and oppressive, as too exclusive and judgmental. It is an attack that is not new; it began with the Enlightenment and continues unabated. It is justified on some levels. In the end, however, it will reach a dead end, and as always we will reach into our distant past for wisdom for our future.

In my undergraduate and graduate teaching, as well as in my work with pastors and in congregations, I find that the dualism between church and world which preoccupied Mennonites even thirty or fourty years ago is largely unknown or irrelevant. We are surrounded by and have been shaped by contemporary culture on all levels. In this situation we can no longer assume a monolithic reading of the Bible, of our history, of present culture. We live in a world that lacks theological and cultural cohesion. We live in a Mennonite church that lacks cohesion. It is the loss of cohesion that characterizes modern and, even more so, post–modern culture. We can no longer delude ourselves into believing that we can isolate ourselves from other traditions, ignore the diverse readings of our own origins and traditions, escape the influence of major theological trends around us, and so on.

I have come to believe, however, that precisely in this period of fragmentation a reinterpretation of the biblical and early Christian doctrine of God is not only possible but urgent for all Christians, including Mennonites, as a way not of avoiding but of handling diversities and distinctives. It is my conviction that we need spiritual and moral renewal not by deconstructing and replacing the classical doctrine of God with a novel one, but by rereading the Bible, classical history and Anbaptist history to find things there that we have overlooked. For instance, our Mennonite view of discipleship, peace, and social justice might possibly be more fruitfully grounded in the mystical, sacramental, and *Gelassenheit* thought of certain Anabaptists than in the harsher obedience-oriented thought of others.

I believe that the best in Anabaptist-Mennonite theology can and ought to be enframed by a classical trinitarian theology in which: (1) God as transcendent creator and mystery of the world is wholly free of our own moral systems, including our own Mennonite view of nonviolence (God is not a pacifist); (2) Christ as eternal *logos* and sophia takes on flesh in Jesus of Nazareth who, through his birth, life, teachings, ministry, death, resurrection, and ascension redeems us (though him we have been and are being saved from our sins) and shows us an alternate way of peace and reconciliation; and (3) the Holy Spirit as the very spirit of God and the very spirit of Christ is present to the whole world and to us as Christians, empowering us and leading us into ever greater freedom–freedom to think new thoughts and find new answers to our existential concerns and moral dilemmas.

III

Yes and No: Conversational Responses

Goshen College not China: Challenges to Mennonite Ethics

Ted Koontz

One of the most attractive and unusual things about J. Lawrence Burkholder's writing and speaking is the combination of lived faith experience and theological reflection. There are, of course, many who live out their faith with marvellous integrity. And there are others who speak and think theologically with eloquence and depth. But there are not many who combine the two as engagingly as he does. One has the sense of a man who always is seeking to apply his faith to life struggles he faces, and one who does not hesitate to pose uncomfortable, life-produced, questions for his faith. While Burkholder certainly has the ability to write, and has written theology which is not explicitly linked to his life story, seeing his theology and lived experience together surely illuminates and gives power to both. His life and thought provide us with an admirable example of action based on faith combined with reflection on faith informed by experience.

Indeed, one of the central challenges which Burkholder poses for Mennonite thought is to come to grips honestly with our experience. The failure to do so, as he saw it, is what most distressed him when he returned to Goshen after China. We would be immeasurably enriched if we could follow his example of honest encounter between theology and life--and if our lives sometimes took us out of our comfortable settings which may seem to pose few obviously hard "dilemmas."

It is in Burkholder's earnest attempt to live his faith authentically that he encounters central problems with the kind of Mennonite theology and ethics he imbibed as a youth. Yet, likely due mainly to the circumstances of his early pastorate (World War II and an articulate Christian gunsmith), he did not simply replicate the faith in which he was nurtured. He went beyond it in at least one crucial respect. On one level it is this going beyond that caused his problems. He went beyond his heritage by seeking to apply his Mennonite ethic "out there," in the world, among those who did not profess Christ as Lord. Life in India and China was life in the "world" at its most raw. Burkholder sought to be nonresistant, not in a stable community in Pennsylvania but in war-torn China. He sought to give the cup of cold water, not where an occasional beggar asked for it but where everyone desperately needed it. He sought to forgive seventy times seven, not where it would seldom if ever be necessary and where it

Ted Koontz is Associate Professor of Ethics and Director of Peace Studies at Associated Mennonite Biblical Seminaries in Elkhart, Indiana.

wouldn't really hurt anybody else if he did forgive, but where people routinely lied and cheated, and where, when they did, others died because of it. Even more, he sought to do all this not on behalf of himself or a group holding his same commitments, but first on behalf of a divergent group of Christian agencies and then on behalf of the United Nations.

In a sense, what is surprising about Burkholder's story is not that he had great difficulty applying his Mennonite ethic in China, but that he seems surprised he had such difficulties! Didn't his traditional Mennonite community teach him the fundamental "fact" (so I would think they would have conceived it) that the "world" was fallen, that it operated on principles other than those which govern life for Christians, that it would be futile, impossible, to "run things" in the world on the basis of Mennonite nonresistant principles? I could imagine (I don't know if it happened) H.S. Bender and Guy Hershberger listening to Burkholder's China stories, seeing fully the "dilemmas" he faced, agreeing fundamentally with his analysis of his situation there, and still feeling no real challenge to Mennonite theology. What he was telling them was nothing new. The world is nasty, it is fallen, it cannot be run "Christianly." This was no challenge to Mennonite theology but rather a confirmation of it.

If there was a challenge in what Burkholder was saying in his China stories, it might have been to accept "responsibility" for the fallen world, a challenge which was made more forthright and potent in his doctoral dissertation. But this was a challenge which his stories may have made his listeners even less likely to want to pick up because doing so may have seemed self-evidently futile. After all, if an intelligent, deeply committed Mennonite like Burkholder ran into such hopeless dilemmas, his experience could surely have been read as reason for a certain kind of "withdrawal," rather than for more involvement or for a modified ethic. A logical response to his experience should have been to focus more attention on a model of world transformation which works at creating an alternative community (light, city set on a hill) rather than on a model which pushes for deeper engagement in the existing structures of the world (leaven, salt). So while Burkholder felt his experiences in China as challenges to the theology which Hershberger and others held at Goshen, I can see how those same experiences could have been read as a confirmation of it, at least in some important respects.

These observations lead to the following question. Does the fact that Burkholder's experiences in China seemed a challenge to his theology mean that, at least on the important question of whether or not we should assume Christian ethics are applicable in a simple, direct way to the fallen "world," he was more like the liberal pacifists of the time than like his fellow Mennonites, especially in the (Old) Mennonite Church, when he went to China? Leading Mennonites of various theological stripes (including Hershberger, Don

Smucker, and John R. Mumaw[1]), were at that time calling themselves "nonresistants" in order to clearly and sharply differentiate themselves from "pacifists" who held just the sort of notions about the efficacy of directly applying Christ's teaching as policy for the world which Burkholder, through his China sojourn, discovered did not work. On at least one level, I think, there is no disagreement between him and those like Bender and Hershberger who seemed to disagree sharply–all believed that "nonresistance" could not be in any simple way applied in that world. There were disagreements, of course, especially over whether one should try to apply it "out there" even if it had to be applied "complexly" rather than "simply," or whether one should withdraw in order to create another community that could live in a more straightforward way by the gospel ethic.[2] But despite these sorts of differences they shared a pessimistic reading of what could be expected in the "world"–and a very similar view of what the gospel ethic required. This is to say that, at least in some important respects, a traditional, "dualistic" Mennonite theology could rather easily answer the challenge Burkholder brought with him from China–which is not to say that the answers and the perspective do not have serious problems.

What posed the hardest challenge for this kind of Mennonite theology was not Burkholder's experience in China but his description of Goshen College. What he is claiming, if I understand him correctly, is that the same dynamics that were at work in China were and are at work in Goshen, though in a somewhat (sometimes, dramatically) moderated way. The situation is not so desperate at Goshen and therefore people are more polite, more considerate. But the difference between China and Goshen, between the world and the church, in Burkholder's view is one of degree, not one of kind. At Goshen as well as in China, power is wielded over others, the welfare of others is in the hands of "higher ups," decisions are made hierarchically, "interests" are weighted, interest groups are formed and stick up for themselves, and so forth. In his description of Goshen College Burkholder is challenging Mennonite tradition not only by arguing that Mennonite Christians should take responsibility for the world, with all the ambiguity his China experience tells him this will involve, but by arguing that the same problems, the same ambiguities, the same *dilemmas*, exist inside the church. They cannot be avoided by avoiding the world. One might summarize by paraphrasing a common saying about identifying the enemy: Burkholder "saw the world, and it was us."

The problem here, in Burkholder's view, is not that administrators et al. are

1 Hershberger argues this in his book *War, Peace, and Nonresistance*; Mumaw in *Nonresistance and Pacifism;* and Smucker in "A Mennonite Critique of the Pacifist Movement," *Mennonite Quarterly Review*, January 1946.

2 This is an important difference. Somewhere along the line Burkholder came to have much more "aggressive" or "positive" outreaching conception of what Christian love meant than was true for many Mennonites.

evil, or sub-Christian. Their intentions may be perfect, but they will face dilemmas; they need to "compromise." The problem is "ontological," embedded in the structure of reality, not in the good or ill will of individuals. As soon as there are two or more neighbors for whom we are to care, we *cannot* unambiguously, simply, follow the ethic of Jesus. The implication of this argument is that Mennonites have been wrong in claiming that the Christian gospel offers a *social* ethic, at least one in any sense resembling what they have thought it offered. Mennonites, as I have suggested, have been less bold than liberal pacifists in claiming that Christian faith offers an ethic which can be readily utilized for running the "world." But Mennonites have always insisted that the ethic of Christ is not only a personal or private ethic.[3] Rather, it is an ethic for a society, namely (at least) the society of those who acknowledge Christ as Lord. This society, they have claimed, is to be governed by gospel norms such as forgiving seventy times seven, nonresistance, putting others' interests above our own. There has never been, at least in serious versions of this view, any pretension that these standards will be lived out perfectly. But to say that we fail to fully live up to these standards is different than to say that they simply are "ontologically" impossible–irrelevant, except as a kind of ideal toward which we are drawn.

I don't know yet if I agree with Burkholder in arguing, if I understand him correctly, that there is no *essential* difference between church and world–that the *essential* difference is between a person, free from the encumbrances of social roles and responsibilities which imply conflicting obligations, and a person encumbered by them and, along with that person so encumbered, organizations of all sorts. Is our social life inherently, ontologically, less capable of being fully Christian than our personal lives–indeed not even appropriately judged by the same norms? I don't have the answer, but I see it is a crucial question which I am especially interested in exploring in relation to church institutions–colleges, mission agencies, hospitals, and the like. Does our Mennonite version of Christian faith tell us anything relevant about how we conceive and run our institutions? *Are* our institutions qualitatively different from other institutions in our society? Perhaps more important, *can* they be, *should* they be? What norms ought we to use in judging them, in running them? If my understanding of Burkholder is right, and if he is right, we have a lot of

3 This, I would contend, is a central theme of continuity running through Mennonite throught and practice from the Anabaptists to the Amish, to John Yoder's *The Politics of Jesus*, and to "liberationist" Mennonites. All have rejected the notion that the radical gospel and its ethic applies only to "personal" morality as much of mainstream Christian ethics has essentially claimed, in one way or another, from Augustine to Luther to Reinhold Niebuhr. Whether or how the gospel ethics can apply to the wider world may be a source of some debate among Mennonites, especially recently, but Mennonites have assumed that the ethic of Jesus can and does apply to the corporate life of the church, not only to the lives of individual Christians.

theological revisioning to do, which will take us into closer fellowship with most other Christian groups.

However these questions are resolved, one of Burkholder's many contributions to me is the gift of this intellectual, theological, and very practical agenda. How can our ethics, or can our ethics, apply to our lives together in institutions run by the church? The attempts in recent decades among Mennonites to speak prophetically to the structures of the world, to speak in ways which call upon them to at least approximate the values of God's reign, seem to me to lack credibility unless we find ways of applying those values in our own corporate, institutional lives. If Burkholder is right, we need either to stop criticizing them or to criticize them in different ways on different grounds. If Burkholder is wrong, we need to empower our institutions to live in ways which prove him wrong. Only then can our prophetic words be authentic, and only then can our gospel be visible in our corporate, institutional lives.

Into Sarajevo: Where Ambiguity Meets Responsibility

N. Gerald Shenk

Several years ago, soon after French President Mitterand flew bravely into Sarajevo under the guns of Serbian siege, offering to send some one thousand more troops to help guard international relief efforts, someone pointedly asked me: What can Christians do in such a situation? Wistfully I offered to lead one thousand Mennonites into beleaguered Bosnia as peacemakers. Wouldn't it be wonderful, we might speculate, if even a small part of the energies spent until now on training for war (or policing) efforts were devoted instead to serious preparation of forces for resolution of violent conflicts?

What makes this speculation wistful, of course, is the painfully obvious reality that neither nations nor churches are inclined or accustomed to mobilizing their resources for peacemaking on a scale even faintly resembling the totalities of modern warfare. Symbolic gestures, even strident protests, humanitarian relief, and genuine efforts to bind up the wounds of war are entirely appropriate, unless they yield enough satisfactions to relieve the pressures for solutions on a broader scope. "We sent the blankets and the medicines; why don't they just stop all that fighting?" To which the Bosnian Muslim hiding in the ruined apartments of Sarajevo retorts: "They keep feeding us so the Serbs can keep on slaughtering us!"

Were it not for the haunting echoes of contemporary realities ringing throughout our retrospective of the life and thought of J. Lawrence Burkholder, it would be tempting to reduce his account to simple contrasts: the agonies of war versus the comforts of civil peace; the satisfactions of tangible relief achievements amid messy emergency situations versus the luxury of academic, ideological purity far removed from the fray; and the burdens of conscientious exercise of institutional power versus the simplicity of separatist refusal to participate in legal and bureaucratic entanglement with the things of this world. Burkholder's thought and action represent a prolonged argument with other powerful voices in the generation that presided over an unprecedented amount of change in the Mennonite communities of North America following World War II.

Those Mennonites who emerged from that war with a heightened sense of opportunity and responsibility toward the society around them, and those who

N. Gerald Shenk is Associate Professor of Church and Society of Eastern Mennonite Seminary in Harrisonburg, Virginia.

abandoned rural and agricultural settings to take up professional and business careers, have a special interest in the insights which Burkholder has elaborated during an illustrious career within and beyond Mennonite programs and institutional settings. Moral ambiguities and ethical dilemmas crop up in unpredictable array, with implications and consequences hard to envision within the framework of first-century and sixteenth-century theological or political agendas alone.

Would that each generation had an abundance of heroes formed in the crucible of response to extreme crises, in the humbling encounter with human limitations stretched beyond recognition by the brokenness of the world in the worst of its modern predicaments and traumas.

But do we really want to live with heroes returned from such encounters to our quiet, settled communities? Can we handle the stature conferred by encounters with great hazards out there somewhere? We are, after all, in many ways still a folk, and folk heroes are always getting reduced a notch or two, taken down to size so they don't get out of hand. Simply to come home from heroic exploits in the netherworlds of politics and dire straits does not necessarily qualify the heir of Anabaptist visionaries to assume responsibility and leadership in our own programs.

Attending to Burkholder's reflections, we detect (along with his justifiable satisfactions in a job done well) the invidious comparison with peers in the Concern circle: some earned their spurs working hard in the real world, while others got to sit at the feet of master European teachers. Long before his reference to Mary and Martha, we sense the frustration of an accomplished task-oriented manager surrounded by the rhetoric of ideologues bent on the disenchantment of once-sacred and unquestionable institutional churchly realities.

There is irony in this lament: a powerful functionary (president of a church college) denied the pleasure of approval even for conscientious stewardship of responsibilities; an ideological monopoly at Goshen on interpretations of the Anabaptist heritage, preventing wider publication of the dissertation which earned highest academic honours at Princeton; and innocence lost at the edges of human civilization (in a mad evacuation scramble requiring force to clear the plane for takeoff), matched only by bewilderment upon discovering that Mennonites profess to reject power and exalt weakness, even while gradually accommodating in order to compete effectively in the modern world.

Yet the purpose of a retrospective is not so much to put the stamp of evaluation on disputes from the past. It might be more instructive to ponder the question, When would you really wish you had a J. Lawrence Burkholder on your team today? What will his approach look like in this generation? Let us not diminish the weight of choice faced at the extremities of human life in previous eras, but surely we ourselves will not escape similar bewilderment in the face of the ambiguities, dilemmas, and traumas inflicted by humans on other humans. Every generation must face itself in defining moments of agony over evil: Guernica, Warsaw, Auschwitz, Hiroshima, My Lai, Kampuchea, Shatilla, Vukovar, Sarajevo . . . . Steady and insistent, the beat goes on, battering us toward fatalistic resignation. What can one person do? What good would Christians and churches offer in such situations? How does hope survive?

I will take personal encouragement from the example set forth over the decades of Burkholder's experiments in reluctant responsibility, acknowledging the ambiguities and the costs of decision-making. And if I could take a team of Mennonites into the jaws of despair encircling Sarajevo today, I would be grateful for the accompaniment of one such as J. Lawrence Burkholder, with his generous view of Christians taking responsibility amid chaos, disruption, and breakdown of civil order in a world run amok. Even small acts of charity and faithfulness will implicate us directly in the confrontation with the powers of evil, if the church is to be the church today. The Anabaptists would not be surprised.

Jesus as Absolute Norm? Some Questions

Gordon D. Kaufman

J. Lawrence Burkholder has given us a moving portrait of a young American Mennonite "innocent abroad," and the consequences his experiences had for his thinking about the meaning of Christian faith and the Mennonite interpretation of that faith. Many of us in Burkholder's generation experienced similar sorts of challenge, during and after World War II, to our more or less traditional Mennonite understandings of Christian faith and life. But for most of us these questions did not arise in the context of experiences that tested in such a wrenching way our convictions about nonresistance, helping those in need, loving neighbor and enemy. I know of no account of those times of testing and rethinking of basic Mennonite convictions that is as thoughtful and insightful as what Burkholder has laid out before us on the basis of his early experiences in India and China. All who value deeply the Mennonite heritage and are puzzled about its meaning for today's world are much indebted to him for these reflections.

I shall not make any attempt here to lift up and comment on Burkholder's many important insights into the dilemmas in which Mennonites today find themselves as they seek to live as responsible Christians in the modern world. His thoughtfulness about these matters speaks loudly and clearly in his "Autobiographical Reflections." Persons deeply concerned about issues of this sort could scarcely do better than to meditate on this text, for it brings out very well many of the major issues. What I would like to do is look briefly at one of the presuppositions of Burkholder's Mennonite stance which remains unexamined in his account; in this way I hope to move our collective reflection on the significance–and the problematical character–of our common Mennonite heritage one step further.

Burkholder is concerned repeatedly in his paper with the difficulty–indeed, the impossibility!–of fulfilling the utterly absolutistic demand of Jesus' emphasis on love of neighbor and of enemy (as Mennonites have understood these matters). He has suggested that a refusal to straightforwardly recognize this problem has led Mennonites into various sorts of hypocrisy, dishonesty, prejudicial judgment of other Christians, and the like, as well as to a widespread failure to carry out quite proper Christian responsibilities in the social and political orders within which we live. Instead of demanding absolute purity and

Gordon D. Kaufman is retired from Harvard Divinity School as Mallinckrodt Professor of Divinity, Emeritus.

perfection in the very impure and imperfect, ambiguous and complex, world in which we live, Mennonites need to understand (he argues) that "compromise" of various sorts is always unavoidable, and this consciousness needs to be given much more prominence in the Mennonite conception of Christian faith than has traditionally been done. In this respect Mennonites have some things to learn from Calvinistic and Lutheran interpretations of Christianity, things which will contribute a good deal to their ability to express a genuinely Christian ethic of love in work and life in today's world.

This counsel is certainly all well taken. Mennonites have been much too simplistic and naive in their understanding of the absolutistic demands of the love-ethic which they have sought to make central to Christian faith and life, and the personal experiences which Burkholder recounts for us demonstrate this sharply and clearly and with great poignancy. But, in view of precisely these difficulties which he sets forth with such cogency, I find it surprising that he nowhere asks some questions about the validity and the appropriateness of this very idea of an absolutistic standard, as well as about the validity and appropriateness of the traditional Mennonite assumption that we actually possess (in and through the Bible) such an absolutistic standard. "I seldom doubted," he says, "the validity and the authority of the eschatological vision."[1] It is not difficult to see why, on traditional Christian grounds, such Mennonite beliefs could easily arise and be taken to be at the very heart of the Christian message. For Jesus Christ was viewed as, in an almost literal sense, the very Son of God, the Word of God which had created the world alive here in the flesh (John 1), the presence of the *Absolute* right here in our midst. So it was thought appropriate and necessary for the faithful to regard Jesus' every word as the absolute truth from on high. The moral demands so central in Jesus' teaching were to be taken, in all their apparent absoluteness, as nothing less than God's direct command to every person. It has been the distinctive mark of Mennonites to take all these matters very seriously, indeed literalistically; and it is hardly surprising, therefore, that they came out with such an utterly absolutistic–and, as Burkholder says, "impossible"–understanding of the Christian love-ethic.

The presupposition of this sort of interpretation was, of course, the traditional dualistic picture of the human situation–a picture according to which "this world" is seen in sharp contrast with an "other world," "nature" is distinguished from "supernature," God is thought of as "in heaven" (as Karl Barth emphasized) while we are here "on earth," etc. And it is in the person of Jesus Christ ("two natures in one person" [Chalcedon]) that these two worlds come together, the absolute God appearing here clothed in the flesh of earth. Many problems, however, arise when one attempts to hold to this traditional supernaturalistic dualism and absolutism in the face of modern understandings

1 J. Lawrence Burkholder, "Autobiographical Reflections," in this volume, 27; cf. 40.

of ecology, evolution, history, sociology, psychology, cultural anthropology, and so forth.[2]

Moreover, it is clear that very few Mennonites have attempted to address these issues directly, examining the ways in which Mennonite interpretations of Christian faith are affected by these problems, and considering the various available ways of dealing with them. I am sure, however, that Burkholder–with his interests in philosophy and in the cultural and intellectual problems with which the modern world confronts Christian faith–must have thought a good deal about these sorts of questions. I am a bit surprised, therefore, that in his reflections he does not even touch on the question whether the message of Jesus is historically conditioned in its formulation, emphases, and content, and thus in significant respects is relative to its time and place (he comes up to the edge of such reflection in a few places.) Also he does not discuss the question of whether the reification of the words of Jesus into absolutistic demands may be a consequence of the failure among Mennonites (going all the way back to Menno himself) to recognize Jesus' own finitude and historicity–thus leading to the inability of many to this day to see what may really be at stake in the central Christian affirmation that Jesus is fully and truly *human*.

If we take this latter quite traditional Christian affirmation seriously, and if we interpret it in light of the compelling modern (as well as post-modern) understandings of human historicity, the question about whether it is really appropriate to think of Jesus' ethical teachings in utterly *absolutistic* terms simply cannot be avoided. But once that point is recognized clearly, many of the problems to which Burkholder addresses himself so forcefully are moved into a somewhat different key. For now we have to frame everything with an eye on Jesus' particular historical situatedness as well as our own. And a central issue for ethics will be the question of the respects, and ways in which what Jesus took to be normative in his historical situation of 2,000 years ago can be applied appropriately to our own situation today.

I am, of course, far from denying that Jesus' teaching, ministry, and crucifixion have significance for our own day (see my discussions of these matters in almost every book I have written); but I do say that a modern historicistic understanding refocuses these matters in important ways. And, I want to emphasize, it calls directly into question Burkholder's claim that the concept of "compromise" provides the best way to address this nest of issues. "Compromise," as he discusses it, seems to presuppose the mistaken notion that we historical beings have *in our possession* an *absolute* standard, since it fails to acknowledge that, however important Jesus' teachings may still be for understanding today's historical situation, they themselves, like everything else

2 For a full discussion of these matters, see my book, *In Face of Mystery: A Constructive Theology* (Harvard University Press, 1993).

in history, are historically conditioned and should not be regarded as straightforwardly "absolute." For an understanding that takes our and Jesus' historicity seriously, therefore, it is not self-evident that the concept of compromise can be particularly helpful in illuminating how Jesus' moral and religious vision should be related to our situation as acting Christians today.

Let me conclude with a speculation about why Burkholder has not been led to pose the issues he discusses in this more historicistic manner. As a General Conference Mennonite, I was struck in reading his paper by the extent to which his experience of Mennonitism and his thinking about Mennonite beliefs have been exclusively bound up with "Old Mennonite" conceptions, writers, and assumptions–bound up with a discourse, that is, which has tended (in my view) to over-emphasize the absolutistic, legalistic, and authoritarian tendencies in our common tradition. (It was, of course, the presence of just such emphases among the "Old Mennonites" that led to the formation of the General Conference Mennonite Church in the first place.) If Burkholder had been more conscious of the existence of real *diversity* in Mennonite views on the issues with which he was concerned (including especially a much greater openness of some toward the secular political order), he might have been led from the beginning to consider other, rather different, ways of interpreting Mennonite absolutism. Perhaps if he had been drafted into Civilian Public Service in World War II–instead of accepting a ministerial classification which permitted him to elect work in India and China under the Mennonite Central Committee–and thus had been exposed in those formative years to other more liberal versions of Mennonite thinking, he might have been led to see his questions about the proper Mennonite role in the wider world in a way not so decisively informed by the narrow absolutism and dogmatism of the Bender/Hershberger/Concern pattern of thinking, a pattern which he quite properly found important to call into question.

But then, of course, we would most likely have been denied this wonderfully insightful story of his own attempts to be a faithful Mennonite in the midst of the ambiguities of modern life! And that would certainly have been a loss to us all.

On Doing Social Ethics: A Personal Response

Duane K. Friesen

I want to thank J. Lawrence Burkholder for sharing his rich and engaging autobiographical reflections from his experience during World War II. Informally, I have often heard "pieces" from that story. By making available the more complete account, he gives us much to ponder. He raises issues that are perennial questions in Christian social ethics. His story of the agonizing and complex decisions Christians faced during that war deserve to be placed alongside the stories of Dietrich Bonhoeffer and the German resistance, and of André and Magda Trocme who risked their lives to save Jews in Le Chambon, France.

By labelling my response "personal" I mean to share from my own perspective where I agree and disagree with how Burkholder thinks about Christian social ethics, and where questions are left unanswered for me. My comments are necessarily brief, and thus cannot be systematically or thoroughly developed. We share common concerns and approaches in three broad areas, as outlined below.

1. Compassion to the neighbor is the heart of Burkholder's ethic. Compassionate service implies meeting the needs not only of individual persons in our care but of aggregates of people who suffer from the neglect of the family, education, and economic and political structures. My spouse, who teaches in the public schools, works with increasingly larger numbers of children who are growing up in the context of poverty and neglect. While their needs are addressed by her individually in the classroom, Christian responsibility only begins there. Love of the neighbor requires that we address issues of public policy which have a profound effect on the lives of these children.

Driven by the logic of Christian compassion to meet basic human needs, Burkholder appropriately accepted a service assignment that involved work within political structures in China during and after World War II. The drive to meet human needs, and his belief that work within political institutions was the best means to meet these needs, outweighed his natural Mennonite hesitation to enter the grey world of politics, where he faced an ambiguity and complexity he had not known and for which he was not prepared.

Duane K. Friesen is Professor of Bible and Religion at Bethel College, North Newton, Kansas.

I concur with him that Mennonites should see politics as a calling, as an arena of service, as an extension of the church's ministry to the world. Many Mennonites would agree with him in the part of the world where I live. I think of two of my friends, James Juhnke on the Bethel College faculty, who ran for Congress in 1970, and Duane Goossen, a member of Goessel Mennonite Church, who is presently a member of the Kansas House of Representatives.

2. I also agree with Burkholder that some of the current trends in Mennonite theological thinking tend to undermine the endorsement of politics as a legitimate Christian vocation. The "theologically correct" emphasis on the church as the starting point for Mennonite social ethics has led to the tendency to support a counter-cultural and almost apolitical stance. Some Mennonite theologians have accepted too uncritically the position of Stanley Hauerwas, who emphasizes an "ethic of character" and calls on the church first of all "to be the church."

But what does it mean to be the church? Certainly it means in part for the church to be an example by the way the members care for each other and by the virtues they exhibit as they live out the Christian story. But the church is also the church when its members scatter in their various places of employment and practice the professions within the institutions of our society, and within political and economic life. The church can also be the church when Mennonites work with others in voluntary associations that seek to bring about change in society, and when Mennonites run for office and seek to propose policies that meet the basic needs of human beings, as well as when they seek to write laws and administer laws to meet these needs.

What does faithfulness mean in those contexts? Simply to call for the church "to be the church" is not adequate, nor is an ethic of virtue or character. I agree with Burkholder that Christian ethics also must deal with quandaries. How do Mennonites treat issues of justice and fairness in their own institutions, let alone in secular institutions? How does one live a life of compassion in contexts where fellow employees are incompetent and need to be fired from a job? How is conflict resolved when persons do not agree? How are Christians faithful in contexts of organizations whose primary interest is the protection of their own self-interest or the maximization of profit at the expense of other values? How does the church address the ambiguities of power and justice?

Burkholder wanted the church to address these issues when he returned from China, but the church froze him out, and I sense he is still angry about that. He should have been angry. The Mennonite Church pushed issues under the rug rather than face tough questions: the existence of genuine dilemmas, the possibility of "compromise." In his work in China Burkholder confronted the question of the "inevitability of sin" and the need to be thrown back on God's mercy and forgiveness. But to raise those issues sounded too Lutheran, too Niebuhrian, to Mennonites. The irony, as Burkholder points out, is that

Mennonites have paid a high price for the failure to address these tough issues. The radical call to discipleship has in fact been domesticated. We now often start with such a watered down version of the good news of the gospel that we do not even recognize the compromises that we do make. He has a long list of these compromises near the end of his autobiographical statement. We are still hesitant to struggle with the ambiguities and complexities of Christian faithfulness in the world of institutions. I fear Mennonite theologians so readily accept Hauerwas's call to "be the church" and his emphasis on an "ethic of character" because it enables them to evade consideration of the quandaries ordinary Christians face as they seek to be faithful in actual institutions within which they live and work.

In 1963 Burkholder wrote an article in the *Christian Century*, "The Peace Churches as Communities of Discernment," that had a profound effect upon my thinking and that continues to state, I believe, the agenda for the church. In that article he views the church as a community of discernment, as a base for "mission" to the larger society. He advocates a model of the church committed to Christ and engaged in a process of discernment of what faithful obedience means in a culture tempted toward either individualistic pietism or pragmatic secularism. He calls for a creative or pioneering mission to the larger society, determined by the needs of the world and the gifts of the church. He calls particularly for the church to engage in projects to arouse public responsibility. This proposal is still a powerful and relevant model for today.[1]

3. I also share Burkholder's underlying methodology, the dialectic between faith and reason or experience. While Burkholder continued to hold to a biblical vision of faith, he was constantly challenged by his experience of the world, asking about the relevance of Jesus for corporate structures, the dilemma of scarce resources when not everyone can be helped, the overwhelming experience of suffering brought on by systemic evil and natural disaster. For him, biblical faith and human experience mutually affect each other. It seems to me that St. Anselm's notion of "faith seeking understanding" best describes this approach. Burkholder states the outcome of this dialectic of faith and reason:

> When we returned to the U.S. in 1949, I brought back two strong and evidently contradictory convictions. One was that *agape* is the ultimate reality by which all human relations must be judged–*agape*, as free-flowing, unlimited, forgiving, nonresistant, unmerited, unconditional, grace transcending all values as God transcends all else including his own creation. "God is love." I knew of no religious teacher and philosopher who taught

1 J. L. Burkholder, "The Peace Churches as Communities of Discernment," *The Christian Century*, Sept. 4, 1963, 1072f.

> unreciprocating love as did Jesus Christ, and none other embodied *agape* love he as did in his life and especially his death on the cross.
>
> The second conviction was that to work in behalf of the poor in the world, even in the political world, seemed legitimate. I had been called to do the best I could in the field of competing powers and conflicting interests. People had to be fed, clothed, and healed. An avenue of significant effectiveness was to use . . . power for the sake of other people. Responsibility could mean living and working accountably within the framework of the political world.

While I share this basic dialectical methodology, I find the actual description of the content of the faith side of this dialectic problematic. Burkholder distinguishes between "love in its simple purity and in its social and organizational refraction." He says: "By pure love I mean disinterested love, unmixed with anticipated rewards, reciprocations, mutual gratification, and preferences based upon merit."[2] He compares the Good Samaritan to Nygren's concept of *agape* love. He describes an act of kindness as uniquely agapaic because it was "voluntary, personal, direct, discrete, unreciprocating love unmixed by self-regarding motivations."[3] Burkholder distinguishes this love from mutual love and friendship: "*Agape* transcends communal relationships."[4] For Burkholder death on the cross is the perfect symbol of agape: "An important implication of the absoluteness of *agape* is that *agape* love cannot be structured unambiguously, for structure itself generally includes self-regarding implications, defenses, safeguards, lines of exclusion, and sanctions."[5] Thus collective life cannot be run by *agape*. Love is "an *historical possibility* but is at best an *occasional one,* since it cannot be structured without contradiction."[6]

Any corporate structures thus inevitably contradict *agape*. As an example of this contradiction, Burkholder describes his firing an employee who was stealing, whereas he believes *agape* love calls for "infinite forgiveness."[7] Nonresistant agape love seems to fit for interpersonal relationships, but not where the welfare of other people is also involved.[8] For Burkholder, "turn the other cheek" means to absolutely refuse to defend one's own interest. Thus he says that "in many ways [Jesus'] life was not representative of ordinary life,"[9]

2 J. Lawrence Burkholder, "Autobiographical Reflections," in this volume, 8.

3 *Ibid.*, 9.

4 *Ibid.*

5 *Ibid.*

6 *Ibid.*, 10.

7 *Ibid.*, 11.

8 *Ibid.*, 12.

9 *Ibid.*, 19.

because Jesus in no sense participated in structured, institutional life. In short, for Burkholder, Jesus is an anarchist in the root meaning of that term, one devoid of any involvement or interest in human structure and organization. In his description of Jesus and the nature of *agape* love, Burkholder is in the tradition of Ernst Troeltsch and Reinhold Niebuhr, who describe Jesus as "purely religious," without any social ethic. Burkholder's description of Jesus is practically identical to Niebuhr's view of Jesus as developed in the essay, "The Ethic of Jesus and the Social Problem."[10]

I think Burkholder develops a docetic, disembodied Jesus, not nearly like the Jesus I read about in the New Testament. He dismisses Walter Wink's exegesis of the Sermon on the Mount, where Wink points out that Jesus teaches an aggressive nonviolence, though Burkholder offers no argument against Wink's exegesis.[11] Burkholder misses the significance of John Yoder's *The Politics of Jesus*, because Burkholder fails to understand Jesus in his social and political context. Burkholder does not take into account the political dimensions of the triumphal entry, the political significance of the question put to Jesus about taxes, the abrasiveness of the cleansing of the temple, or the clashes with Herod and the religious establishment. In my reading of the New Testament, love is concretely embodied in justice, as in the case of Zacchaeus who, in response to Jesus, redistributes his goods and resources to those who have been wronged. Jesus' love is expressed not only in "infinite forgiveness" but also in harsh judgment.

To define love as self-sacrificing *agape* is to put the cart before the horse. The essence of love is the concern to bring wholeness to human beings, to seek their good, and to restore broken relationships. The essence of love is mutual companionship or friendship. Love expresses itself in doing justice or in seeking justice for others. Justice is thus an extension of love, not a contradiction of love.[12] The self-sacrificing agape is revealed in Jesus' clashes with the "powers that be" in the pursuit of wholeness for people. Sacrificial love is thus a means to human wholeness–the willingness to give our resources, our energies, even our lives for the sake of the well-being of others.

Starting with this norm does not free us from facing many dilemmas, but such

10 Reinhold Niebuhr, *Love and Justice: Selections from the Shorter Writings of Reinhold Niebuhr*, ed. D. B. Robertson. (New York: The World Publishing Company, 1957), 29f.

11 Walter Wink, *Violence and Nonviolence in South Africa* (Philadelphia: New Society Publishers), 1987.

12 See the article by Herbert Richardson, "Martin Luther King–Unsung Theologian," in *New Theology* No. 6, ed. by Martin Marty and Dean Peerman (New York: MacMillan, 1969), 178f. In this article Richardson contrasts the view of love as the pursuit of friendship or wholeness in Martin L. King, Jr. with the concept of self-sacrificing agape in Reinhold Niebuhr. I am essentially following Richardson's argument. A similar argument could be made against the false dichotomy of agape love and philia in the work of Anders Nygren, whom Burkholder also cites for his own view of *agape*.

a norm locates them in a much different arena than Burkholder does. In this view, the use of force is not inevitably a violation of *agape*. Jesus' cleansing of the temple, as an expression of his outrage against the "powers that be," or his pronouncement of judgment on the establishment (without a word of infinite forgiveness), or his proposing to his followers a way to confront their oppressors nonviolently (a third way between passivity and violence–Wink), are ways in which love works in the real world in which we live. God does not call on us to be faithful in some "impossible ideal" world of no structures and institutions; the example of Jesus is really embodied within the structures and institutions of the world. Burkholder's dualism, which views Jesus as someone who spoke to "personal" issues but not "institutional" questions, grows out of a misunderstanding of the nature of love, and results in a docetic view which divorces Jesus from the social and political context of his time.

As I said, we must still face many tough dilemmas. How can nonviolent force be used redemptively? How do we employ scarce resources of time, energy, and material means in the pursuit of justice? How do we express love to a neighbor who is being violated by someone, and at the same time seek the well-being of the neighbor who is doing the violation? What compromises may be made when we work in institutions (both church and non-church) where policies and practices may benefit some, but hurt others? What is the place of benefit/cost calculus in a Christian social ethic?

I find Burkholder's ethic inadequate because it is not comprehensive enough. One cannot develop a Christian ethic simply by looking to Jesus. A Christian social ethic must be grounded in a broader theological framework that includes doctrines of creation, sin, redemption, and eschatology, understood in the light of Jesus Christ. For example, I do not believe an adequate doctrine of creation can sustain an anarchist philosophy: we are created by God as social animals. I have argued elsewhere that such a doctrine will include a positive view of political structures–that the "state," for example, is not simply a remedial institution as a result of sin. Human beings are given responsibility to order their world amidst the diversity and plurality of human culture. The ordering of political and human institutions is indeed complicated and complex, but this task and responsibility is an expression of our love to the neighbor, and is not outside the realm of *agape* love.[13]

Furthermore, Burkholder's social ethic is incomplete because there is no simple way to move from Jesus to political institutions without the development of some kind of middle axioms that bridge the gap between the church and political institutions, and between the community of a shared faith and the

13 For a fuller development of this line of argument, see especially chapter two on creation and sin in my book, *Christian Peacemaking and International Conflict: A Realist Pacifist Perspective* (Scottdale, Pa.: Herald Press, 1986), 49f.

plurality and diversity of worldviews of the larger political community. Burkholder has not told us how he does that.

This leads to a question. What is Burkholder's norm (implicit middle axiom) for the state qua state? I think he answers this question on page 47 of his "Reflections": "My impression is that were one to (1) define pacifism openly as a personal calling while allowing that the state may, indeed must, use police and at least a minimum of military force to fulfill its function; and (2) devote energies to peacemaking in particular by advancing the most rational, imaginative, inexpensive, minimal uses of force, the response of the public would not be automatically negative." In short, the norm for the state is the "just war."

Here we have an old issue that continues to be the subject of endless debates in Mennonite peace theology. Burkholder's position raises a host of questions. What about the character of God? Is God's action with the left hand non-violent within the church, while with the right hand force orders history? What then of the conviction expressed in the book of Revelation that ultimately what triumphs in history is the way of the slain lamb? Do we have a moral relativism here? Is Burkholder saying it is right for Christians inside the church to be personally pacifist, but the state is also morally right when it uses violent force justly? What is the meaning of his distinction between the personal and institutional?

Since Burkholder has defined Jesus as an advocate of a personal ethic, and an anarchist with respect to institutions, then is Jesus irrelevant to the way Christians behave in the corporate structures of politics? What has been gained by Burkholder's position? Do pacifists have anything really to offer within the body politic? Since force is justified, does not the pacifist, then, also need to support the state's preparation for the use of force (including war) so it will be ready when the eventual just war comes about? Further, doesn't this mean the support of "readiness" to meet one's opponent with the most sophisticated technology, given the importance of being able to win a war if the fighting of it should be justified? Hasn't Burkholder given away the store?

I think nonviolent resolution of conflict should be the norm or middle axiom for a pacifist who participates in politics, not just war. A pacifist should bring to her participation in politics a commitment to use her imagination, ingenuity and intellect, energy, diplomatic skill, and whatever else to seek a nonviolent resolution to conflict. That is the norm for the state qua state. The resort to the use of force is a sign of the failure of the state to do its job, to order human behavior without violence. I am not so naive as to suggest that violent force will not be used by the state. Its use is an empirical reality in our world. In that context, the pacifist (while continuing to be a gadfly searching for nonviolent solutions) may appropriately hold the state accountable to its own standards: is the use of force a last resort, or have nonviolent alternatives been ignored; are the means used restrained and limited, only as much as necessary to restore the peace; are non-combatants sufficiently protected in the course of the use of force? The reader will recognize here the standard criteria of just war theory. My difference from Burkholder's position is that I do not grant these standards as a legitimate norm for the state. The norm for the state is nonviolence. This standard derives from the character of God as revealed in Jesus Christ which is the key to *all* reality, and thus the standard for all institutions. This position is, I take it, what is meant by the affirmation of the Lordship of Christ over both church and world, or what is meant by saying that the Kingdom of God (God's rule over the entire cosmos) is made manifest most supremely in Jesus Christ.

Finally, I conclude with some reflections on the status of autobiographical statements such as Burkholder's. The rich experience shared there here helps us put flesh on our abstractions, keeps us in touch with reality, and helps us face the "harder" dilemmas of life without quick and easy solutions that don't touch the ambiguity of human existence. Having said that, the fact that a person has had the kind of experience that others have not had does not mean that his *interpretation* is thereby more true or ethically correct. To appeal authoritatively to one's own experience as a basis for the *validation* of one's interpretation of that experience is an ad hominem argument. I am not saying that Burkholder himself engages in ad hominem, but simply warning those who read his account not to accept his interpretation just because he had this experience and we who critique his position did not. We show our respect for him by engaging him in the kind of vigorous discussion he missed when he returned from China in 1949. Our engagement with his ideas is long overdue.

Which Jesus? Alternatives to the Ethics of Compromise

John Richard Burkholder

My assignment for the Sunday morning session at the Laurelville conference was to wrap up the whole event. That required taking into account not only J. Lawrence Burkholder's autobiographical statement and his further spoken reflections, but also the prepared papers from three other theological viewpoints and the lively ensuing dialogue. Writing about this experience for a different audience some months later, I realized that it is impossible to recapture the spontaneous energy of the time together. I can only offer a few suggestions and questions to further an ongoing conversation.

Since an important aspect of the presentations at Laurelville was autobiographical, I'll indulge in the same mode. These reminiscences, however, are intentionally limited by the conference theme of "conversations with J. Lawrence Burkholder." That is, I'm recounting only those bits of my own story that connect with his, both personally and topically. (Readers should know that, in spite of the similarity of names, our two Burkholder family lines go back to Switzerland independently for at least seven generations. I'm indebted to the genealogical research of Lawrence's father, Henry L. Burkholder, for that knowledge.)

I first met J. Lawrence Burkholder as my instructor in philosophy and ethics at Goshen College in 1950. I had come back to Goshen as a junior, anticipating study with those well-known church leaders H.S. Bender and J.C. Wenger, but it turned out that Burkholder, just a decade older than I, became the teacher who stretched my intellectual horizons and became my prized mentor. Looking back, I now realize that I hadn't yet experienced enough of the "real world" to appreciate the full import of his occasional references to the wrenching dilemmas and ambiguities of his years in China.

Burkholder tells us that he went to China as the moral equivalent of serving the nation in war. Ten years later in 1954, I responded to the call to be a pioneer in the mission advance of the Anabaptist vision. My motivation for becoming a Mennonite missionary in Brazil might be described as an aspiration to fulfil the Goshen ideal of discipleship, amplified by youthful enthusiasm for new frontiers. Brazil challenged my inherited truisms. Although only in my mid–twenties and subject to attacks of Mennonite minority self-consciousness and inferiority, I soon discovered that I was on a more progressive trajectory

John Richard Burkholder formerly taught at Goshen College and is now Adjunct Professor of Peace Studies at Associated Mennonite Biblical Seminaries, Elkhart, Indiana.

than most of the other missionaries at language school. I was appalled by the cultural arrogance and theological narrowness of the typical evangelical. At the same time, I was spiritually overwhelmed by my encounter with the poverty and oppression of the "third world" (although that term hadn't yet come into usage).

Refreshing new insights came from meeting and working with Richard Shaull, who had recently begun teaching at the Campinas Presbyterian Seminary after his forced departure from a decade of controversial social involvement as a missionary in Colombia. Shaull had just finished writing *Encounter with Revolution*, a little book that made its mark as a precursor of liberation theology.[1] Through his guidance I engaged the big questions of injustice, Marxism, and North American imperialism in a theological climate shaped by Karl Barth.

Equipped now with a neo-orthodox concept of grace and some tools of radical social analysis, I began to question the formation I had received at Goshen. The *Concern* pamphlets were beginning to make waves, and I brashly jumped into the dialogue, proclaiming my reaction to the narrow sectarianism (as I then saw it) espoused by John H. Yoder and others. In my sole contribution to the *Concern* forum (a letter published in No. 4, June 1957), I quoted from Paul Verghese, my Goshen College classmate from India. He had concluded one phase of his education in the United States by observing that "at Goshen I found new breadth and meaning to the Christian ethic, but I had to go to Princeton to find new insight into the Gospel."

In the thirty-eight years since those muddled months in Brazil, I have experienced several more paradigm shifts in theology, social theory, and self–understanding. But like Burkholder, I have continued to struggle with the dilemmas of grace and discipleship, of justice and love, of divine power and human weakness, especially my own.

The richness and intensity of the theological conversation at Laureville on that March 1992 weekend evoked new vistas of discernment on those recurring themes. In the remainder of this paper, I will attempt to play back some observations and questions from the provocative clues offered by Lawrence and others.

1. *Character formation.* At one point in the discussion Burkholder was asked why, in the face of all the challenges to his received tradition, he remained a Mennonite. He responded by commending not the foundations of Anabaptist theology but the quality of the peoplehood. He also spoke of the gracious character of his mother, who lived out an *agape* ethic without knowing the term. It appears that underlying all his difficulties with Mennonite leaders and

1 M. Richard Shaull, *Encounter with Revolution* (New York: Association Press, 1955).

institutions is his recognition that the distinctive enduring quality of the Anabaptist-Mennonite witness is the story of a faithful church community. This is what shaped him; it also may be what called him back from the ivy-covered halls of Harvard to the prairies of Goshen. Without a distinct community to nurture and pass on the faith, nothing endures.

But how does one explain the saving graces of that peoplehood? How account for grace-filled lives emerging from the matrix of the narrow, ingrown, legalistic congregational life that Burkholder describes? In our conversation, there was general agreement between Sawatsky, Burkholder, and others that appropriate character formation (*being*) is foundational for proper ethical decision (*doing*). But what do we really know about forming Christian character? It would appear that something from beyond has to be given and received—the gift of inner security, of knowing that one is accepted, both in the community and before God. And that brings us to the basic question of salvation.

2. *Salvation and peace*. At another point Burkholder said, "If I were writing a theology, I'd begin with soteriology and atonement." Allow me to propose a starting point for that theology. A central affirmation must be that God's gracious act of self-giving in the cross of Christ sets us free to love both neighbors and enemies. Classic Christian theology has always claimed that we do not need to keep the law to earn salvation, or be good to escape judgment, or make our own sacrifice to propitiate our guilt. The strange logic of salvation is that the gospel of cross and resurrection frees us from those bondages so that we might live securely, graciously, and unafraid in a hostile world. We cannot save ourselves, and we don't need to. In the mystery of redeeming grace, we sinners are enabled to begin loving our enemies even as God did. "Perfect love casts out fear." Peacemaking is not a burden, but an opportunity made possible by God's liberating action.

3. *Asking the right question*. From this grounding, it becomes possible to explore connections between salvation, ethics and church community. J. Denny Weaver has proposed a three-fold typology of forms of Christian community and their respective social-ethical strategies. Although Weaver's model is triangular, it is grounded in Ernst Troeltsch's classic church-sect typology. Weaver's "withdrawn alternative community" (WAC) and his "socially active alternative community" (SAAC) are variants of the sect type; the "Corpus Christianum" (CC) is, of course, the church type.

We may distinguish the root question for the social ethic of each position as follows:

1. WAC: What ought I do to be pure, holy, unspotted from the world?
2. CC: What ought I do to build, preserve and defend the social order?
3. SAAC: What ought I do to love the neighbor?

This way of putting it illuminates Burkholder's early struggle with the inherited Mennonite ethic. In one of the landmarks of his parents' generation, Daniel Kauffman's *Doctrines of the Bible*, "nonresistance" was categorized along with nonconformity as a "restriction"–how pathetic a label for the central peace dimension of the gospel! Mennonitism was circumscribed by these negative strategies of survival for a withdrawn sect. But when Burkholder moved beyond that self-centered (in the sense of maintaining one's own righteousness) and negative view, he found the tension between positions 2 and 3 more sharply focused. In China, he was forced to consider both the real-life problems and the philosophical dilemmas posed by the necessities of maintaining social order (the CC question) and the unavoidable limits of trying to love too many neighbors.

This tension is inadequately addressed, however, by introducing the categories of ambiguity and compromise. The more basic issue has to do with the distinctive understandings of the meaning of Jesus that inform the models 2 and 3.

4. *Which Jesus*? Underlying much of this whole discussion is a major theological question: What is the relevance of Jesus the Christ as ethical teacher and example? Again and again, Burkholder has bared his soul struggle with the apparently impossible demands of the synoptic Jesus. Questions about perfectionism and obedience dominate his pilgrimage. His quest circles around the question, What really is the functional authority of Jesus' ethic? Are his teachings, especially the hard sayings, intended as serious admonitions to be followed by the faithful, or do they serve primarily to show us our need, to induce guilt and provoke repentance and faith, as in the stereotypical Lutheran model?

This debate has been going on for centuries. How to respond to Jesus' hard sayings was recognized as a crucial problem ever since Clement of Alexandria, or perhaps even since Paul and James. With his concluding eloquent description of the need for "forgiving grace," Burkholder appears to opt for the Lutheran solution, though reluctantly. To the many paradoxes he has already identified, we may add his implicit assumption that the more seriously we take the figure of the historical Jesus, the more irrelevant he becomes for our lives in the world!

If in fact following Jesus is by definition impossible, not just difficult and demanding, then the whole paradigm shifts. We cannot pursue this problem here, but it must be noted that J. Denny Weaver, following John H. Yoder, has set forth an activist sectarian Jesus, one who is socially and politically relevant yet nonviolent. Following this Jesus results in a "messianic community" that engages the world in a way that transcends the forced option of withdrawal or responsibility, creating a social ethic that neither ignores history nor takes responsibility for its outcome.

5. *Burkholder's ethical concepts.* How does an ethic function? Among the various options that appear in the Burkholder story, there is the *ideal* of *agape* love embodied in Jesus, the contrasting *methods* of (deontological) discipleship and (teleological) responsibility, and the *limit* of personal nonresistance. Burkholder has acknowledged that his theology was largely shaped by the prevailing influences of the 1950s, and others of us have confessed our own preferences of sources, periods, and mentors. Is it possible to establish a more creative dialogue between the theological generations? In identifying some of the specific ethical themes in his thought, I want to suggest alternative ways of working at them.

6. *Love and justice.* Burkholder seems to take for granted an absolutist view of agape love, a notion that he learned from Anders Nygren and Reinhold Niebuhr. In this construct, agape is totally self-giving, sacrificial, without any self-regard, leading only to martyrdom and the cross. By definition, it is an impossible ethic, functioning only as an abstract ideal that judges all human effort. But is this what Jesus is really about? Does he demand the obviously impossible? Other biblical and ethical scholars (e.g., Marcus Borg, Victor Furnish, William Klassen, Gene Outka) speak of love as compassion, as caring, as equal regard for self and others. From these other perspectives, an ethic of love is still demanding, but not by definition impossible.

Again, recent biblical scholarship has recovered a view of *justice* grounded in the prophets that is distinct from the Graeco-Roman legal model of *suum cuique* adopted by Burkholder in the 1950s. Although one need not accept all of José Miranda's persuasive and rigorous reinterpretation of the justice/righteousness language (see his *Marx and the Bible*[2]), a clear demand for radical social reordering is at the heart of the Bible. "Seek first God's kingdom and his justice" serves as a motif for a social ethic that posits just order as the goal, with nonviolent compassion ("love") as the means.

7. *Responsibility.* At the start of his story Burkholder struggles with the claim that "if Hitler were to prevail, I would be responsible." This haunting shadow shapes the whole narrative, and of course social responsibility becomes the focus of the 1958 dissertation.

But with all due respect for his sensitivity to the challenge thrust upon him, formidable questions about the meaning of responsibility remain. *To whom* are Christians responsible? And *for what*? Simply to urge that sectarians become "responsible" does not resolve the dilemmas of competing loyalties. How do we order the priorities of responsibility to family, nation, church, humanity—or

2 José P. Miranda, *Marx and the Bible: A Critique of the Philosophy of Oppression* (Maryknoll: Orbis Books, 1974).

God? In the face of the Nazi threat, who was more faithfully responsible: Dietrich Bonhoeffer or the villagers of Le Chambon who risked their lives to shelter Jewish refugees?

Reinhold Niebuhr's persuasive way of stating the problem is not the only option. Stanley Hauerwas, Charles Scriven, and John Yoder offer compelling critiques of the "Christian realist" view of responsibility that seems to dominate Burkholder's thinking.

8. *Compromise.* Throughout his narrative Burkholder concedes the necessity of facing ambiguities and compromises in concrete ethical decisions. But it is unfair to assume that he adopted "compromise" easily; rather, his keen moral sensitivity saw inevitable dilemmas in applying the perfectionist ethic of Jesus to complex human situations. The unfortunate gap between Burkholder and the leaders at Goshen was more than a generation gap. His profound *experience* in the torment of China marks the crucial differentiation from the church fathers. Their theology was shaped largely in the safety of libraries, his in the China crucible where he had been forced to make agonizing decisions far from tranquil Mennonite communities.

Surely it is lamentable that Burkholder's probing voice was silenced a generation ago, not only for the personal pain that he experienced, but also because the fundamental questions focused by his critique were officially sidelined for years. It appears that no one was able to provide satisfactory answers to his actual China dilemmas, such as whether or not to force refugees off an over-crowded plane so that at least some could be rescued. Mennonite ethics can no longer ignore the questions that Lawrence has raised so acutely. Issues of ambiguity, compromise, social responsibility, and above all the uses of *power* demand sustained critical and faithful attention.

9. *Language, truth, and God.* Although Burkholder's presentation did not address basic theological questions, at several points the conversation was pushed toward ultimate issues. Intense interchanges about the use of language and the meaning of symbols exposed profound differences in both theological assumptions and conclusions.

In conclusion, I am profoundly grateful for J. Lawrence Burkholder's contribution to the Mennonite church, to society, and not least to my own life. I commend his incisive exposure of the contradictions and avoidances in so much of Mennonite preaching and practice. I resonate with his call to discerning political involvement. And above all I deeply appreciate his personal candor and humility in expressing his soul struggles with the persistent dilemmas of faith and obedience.

IV
Concluding Postscript

Concluding Postscript

J. Lawrence Burkholder

With this appendix to the second edition of *The Limits of Perfection*, I am given an opportunity to express my appreciation to the editors. That Rodney Sawatsky and Scott Holland have found my "Autobiographical Reflections" worthy of publication is most gratifying. And for the editors to have solicited responses from various Mennonite scholars is equally audacious and generous. The Laurelville weekend, after all, was designed for informal conversation rather than for the publication of prepared statements on announced topics. I hope that readers will allow its *ad hoc* qualities of spontaneity and uncalculated personal expression to compensate for its impressionistic character. The essays, though disparate in intent, are all kindred in spirit, and I wish to thank each respondent for his contribution. I would also express appreciation to Arnold Snyder of Pandora Press for publishing this second edition.

How does one bring a conversation to a close? Certainly not by saying the last word. Conversations close when time runs out, or when someone poses an unanswerable question, or when someone falls asleep! It would be tempting for me to reply to each respondent separately. In that way I could distinguish between my earlier perceptions as an "innocent abroad" and reflections which may have benefited by graduate education and later experience. I would enjoy correcting certain misinterpretations of my point of view. But my guess is that readers would be less than enthralled by my turning a discussion into a debate. So I have decided simply to make a few remarks in the spirit and tradition of *A Concluding Unscientific Postscript*. After all, we have been discussing an "enduring problem": how to live the Christian life in a changing world. Specifically, I have decided to limit these comments to an amplification of a few ethical concepts, some of which are not typically Mennonite but which, I believe, may receive additional coinage as Mennonites become more deeply involved in the world.

A perceptive student has noted that the structure of my ethics has not changed fundamentally with the years. Whether he was commending me for the stability of my thought or the stubbornness of my spirit was not clear. If he meant that I am somewhat dated, I acknowledge his observation, though I need not insist that everyone in these post-modern days is either dated or soon will be. Furthermore, I would question whether the latest is necessarily the best, as a comparison of Beethoven and Stravinsky would attest. Both are valid but different, though Stravinsky would admit that Beethoven was fundamentally right in the sense that his music represents an indispensable residuum upon which others have drawn.

My ethics were formed, as the autobiographical statement attests, by experiences associated with World War II. Although much has happened since the 1940s that would tend to qualify the stark reality of unbound evil, I cannot erase from my mind that pole of the dialectic for which Hitler and his gas ovens are its Western historical incarnation and the rape of Nanking its Far Eastern equivalent. I was close enough to the dynamics of war and the totalitarian claims of tin men to internalize the mystery of evil as a permanent condition of nature and history. Call it "original sin" with Augustine or "radical evil" with Kant, my expectations for the future have, at any rate, been dampened, except for an eschatological intervention about which we Christians talk but can hardly imagine.

If gas ovens and scorched earth policies are no more, evil, nevertheless, remains even in the chambers of civility, though happily in more subtle and dramatically less destructive forms. So I twinge and sometimes shudder when certain theologians talk about "cultural transformation" as if all that is necessary is one more conference of specialists at worst, or one more prophetic word at best.

Lest I be interpreted as a reactionary conservative, I would remind readers that I have been on the liberal side of most social issues, having spent time in jail with Martin Luther King, Jr. and having demonstrated in Boston's streets against military involvement in Vietnam. All I am calling for is an honest approach to social reality, according to which the possibilities and limits of personal and political ethics are realistically acknowledged.

But my realism applies to the other pole of the dialectic as well. I refer to Jesus' radical, perfectionistic ethic of sacrificial love. Richard Burkholder is right when he insists that the New Testament seems to acknowledge more than one concept of love. I have been aware that the Apostle Paul, especially, was more interested in the multiple forms of communal love than in simply the rational extrapolation of *agape*. As an apostle he adapted love to the cultural situation at places like Corinth and Ephesus while preaching "Christ and him crucified." My own position with respect to the concrete application of the law of love is closer to Paul than to Matthew. But I would insist that adjustment to the complexities of pastoral situations and the conditions imposed by Hellenistic cultures must be seen and evaluated in relation to the ideal of sacrifice. Certainly, *agape* love is not necessarily applicable to all situations, but all applications of love must be measured in relation to self-giving. Some may be surprised to know that even certain Stoics upheld the superiority of self-sacrifice over mutuality. If Gordon Kaufman feels that I am needlessly bound to the authority of Jesus, I would respond by saying that even if there were no Jesus of Nazareth, I would still regard *agape* love as the pinnacle beside which all else are lesser values. As I said in my autobiographical statement, I learned about *agape* from my mother.

My ethics concerns issues having to do with life in its multitudinous manifestations lying between, on the one hand, a dialectic of the demonic which became incarnate in Hitler and, on the other hand, the perfectionistic teachings of Christ. What we are dealing with is an ambiguous world of people, powers, systems, traditions, cultures, and laws, none of which are by their natures consummately good or evil but which in combination make up this vibrant yet somber world. To act concretely and responsibly for the neighbor in the context of a world of unmerited grace and undeserved pain is the mandate of Christian ethics. Today opportunities for service are numerous and of unprecedented variety, as specializations are made possible through science and the advancement of knowledge. We are living in an ambiguous but serendipitous world.

It may seem almost ridiculous to argue for the reality of moral ambiguity. But Mennonites have resisted ambiguity as a social reality and especially as a category of ethics. To be sure, they have acknowledged that the world out there, especially the political order as distinct from the church, is inevitably a combination of black and white. In recent years, it has been claimed that Christians may give counsel to government by recourse to so-called "middle axioms." The intent would be to encourage governments to operate according to the best possible alternatives without undermining their purpose as agents of force for the sake of order.

But my own inclination is to see organized life in all realms, including Christian communities, as a mixture of good and evil. The "perfection of Christ" as a collective entity is not an historical possibility apart from a total transformation of finite reality. One must acknowledge that the historic Mennonite search for unambiguous living space is not without reason. All of us prefer to live without contradiction, just as a surgeon would avoid an incision where possible. But, unfortunately, it is impossible to do surgery without negative implications through loss of blood, complications, side effects, and the danger of complete failure. In all areas of life, we must weigh the prospects for good against the dangers of evil and make our decisions accordingly. The desire to do good and the willingness to tolerate evil, within limits of course, are inextricably interwoven. This is the experience of reflective businessmen, responsible politicians, sensitive social workers, dedicated administrators, caring pastors, and loving parents. When will we acknowledge that not only governments operate by "middle axioms," but Mennonites do as well? Unless we are to deny the essential conflict between the ethic of Christ and the ordinary presuppositions of civil life, we must acknowledge that all of us compromise as the only way to get anything done. It is a matter of where, when, and how much–rather than the principle of compromise as such–that is at issue. Measured against the absolute, any everyday reality inevitably exposes itself as compromise.

With passion, Mennonites have generally denied the necessity of compromise. As soon as compromise is mentioned, American Mennonite scholars are inclined to deflect the issue by simply attributing such thought to the influence of Reinhold Niebuhr, as if he were the author of the idea. In reality, I have been influenced more by St. Augustine and Ernst Troeltsch than by Reinhold Niebuhr. Troeltsch, a relativist, used the term "Kompromiss" to represent the transition from the absolute to the relative. Compromise, though ambiguous, is not to be regarded as a pact with the devil but the condition under which Christianity can endure. Compromise is a principle by which Christianity has been able to adjust to changing situations from century to century. It is a necessary presupposition of mission.

Of course, there have always been purists who see almost any accommodation to existing structures as unfaithfulness in principle. But unless we are to conclude that all must be homeless itinerants, as many of the early disciples were, we must allow Christians enough leverage to live as settled communities in the context of power, law, reciprocity, hierarchical structures, competition, institutional establishments, political responsibility, and social give-and-take in many forms. This is not to ignore or repudiate the radical ethic of Christ, but to call attention to the obvious fact that systems of the world in which Christians are placed do not, indeed cannot, operate by selfless giving alone. All corporate structures, even "nonresistant" Hutterite colonies, either defend themselves or call upon others to do so for them, whether through insurance companies, cooperatives, professional associations, legal authorities, or police powers. Today even church organizations are so caught up in binding commitments to patrons, policies, precedents, and legalities that they define the policies of their operations as much in terms of enlightened self-interest as of loving vulnerability. Even benevolent institutions, which exist to serve humanity and are essential to humanization processes, are ambiguous.

It has been my experience to observe that most Mennonite entrepreneurs, physicians, business experts, and administrators know very well that there is a conflict between the ideals of discipleship and the reality of their situations. Many, of course, lack the theoretical language by which to understand their situations. Hence, references to Christian ideals of purity, nonresistance, turning the other cheek, and the ethics of Anabaptist martyrdom tend to make them feel guilty. Therefore, the question is, How can they be comforted, if not encouraged, without unwittingly confusing the principles of civil morality by which they operate with the perfection of Christ? I feel that the way to do this is to set forth a dialectical framework according to which the ideal and the real are clearly differentiated, even though mixed in ambiguous situations. Frankly, I would rather live in tension than to redefine the terms of the ethical situation in a manner which may make one feel good but would really be dishonest. In other words, I will not allow such terms as love and justice, nonresistance and nonviolence, the righteousness of the Sermon on the Mount and conventional morality, the ethics of the church and the ethics of the political order, the ultimate and the penultimate, to be melted into a paste of innocuous social glue. To be sure, social reality is a mixture of all of these. But to insist upon distinctions born of a dialectical method of thinking may have the advantage of protecting the ideal against profanation by identifying it with the systems of this world.

At the present time, some Mennonite ethicists are attempting to avoid the logic of ambiguity, lesser evil, and tragic necessity by abandoning the language of classical Christianity, which once served Mennonite polemics against Christendom but which has begun to boomerang. Once we could criticize the rich simply for being rich, mayors for the use of power, financial agents for selling insurance, Christian politicians for being political, and institutions for being institutions.

But now, since we are involved in all of these things, the polemic has changed from one of principle to one of the misuse of power and injustices of all kinds. It is now assumed that by being careful, one can participate in the competing structures of power without being of those structures. Today Mennonites look for uncompromising ground between the older dualisms of church and world, darkness and light, *agape* love and aggression, legitimate pride and humility, nonresistance and violence. Even "tragic necessity" has been referred to as justification for the use of armed force as an essential component of peacemaking in places like Bosnia. It is generally assumed that out there somewhere lies a "third way" in which Mennonites can participate with impunity. Mennonites no longer want to be separated from the world. Rather, they want to be in it without getting their hands dirty. Obviously, I concur with the tendency among Mennonites to enter the power structures of the world for the sake of good. But the presumption of purity is simply naive.

Finally, my critique assumes the legitimacy and utility of classical Christian language. But now, with the advent of post-modernity, recourse to the terminology of modernity, let alone traditional orthodoxy, is being challenged. Furthermore, recent New Testament scholarship has tended to question the possibility of extrapolating ethical principles from the biblical story. Ethics is becoming increasingly a matter of subjective choice and communal interpretation.

It is tempting, especially for the free churches, to buy into post-modernity in the name of freedom from the rigidities of classical essentialist metaphysics, foundationalist ethics, and the "systems" of the world. It is also tempting to rationalize ourselves out of any dilemma by redefining terms and by rejecting any framework of ethics that ascribes a definite shape to love. It is characteristic of sectarians in trouble to move from form to motive or, to put it otherwise, from pacifism as a concrete response to evil to peace as a universal ideal.

Were the discussion which began with the Laurelville weekend to be resumed, it would be helpful to consider the possibilities of Mennonite language which would account for what my classical Augustinian terminology has tried to express but which may be more acceptable to Mennonites today. That is, I will not die for my language, but I prefer not to be deprived of certain convictions that have marked me for nearly fifty years as a less than fully understood servant of the Mennonite church.

May 22, 1996

Were the discussion which began with the Laurelville weekend to be resumed, it would be helpful to consider the possibilities of Mennonite language which would account for what my classical Augustinian terminology has tried to express but which may be more acceptable to Mennonites today. That is, I will not die for my language, but I prefer not to be deprived of certain convictions that have marked me for nearly fifty years as a less than fully understood servant of the Mennonite church.

May 22, 1996

Were the discussion which began with the Laurelville weekend to be resumed, it would be helpful to consider the possibilities of Mennonite language which would account for what my classical Augustinian terminology has tried to express but which may be more acceptable to Mennonites today. That is, I will not die for my language, but I prefer not to be deprived of certain convictions that have marked me for nearly fifty years as a less than fully understood servant of the Mennonite church.

May 22, 1996

V
Selected Bibliography

Selected Bibliography

J. Lawrence Burkholder

Books and Pamphlets

The Church and the Community. Scottdale, Pa.: Mennonite Publishing House, 1958.

Following Christ in our Work. Study Guide to Guy F. Hershberger, *The Way of the Cross in Human Relations*. Scottdale, Pa.: Mennonite Publishing House, 1959.

The Problem of Social Responsibility from the Perspective of the Mennonite Church. Elkhart, Ind.: Institute of Mennonite Studies, 1989.

Sum and Substance: Essays by J. Lawrence Burkholder. Edward Zuercher, ed. Goshen, Ind.: Pinchpenny Press, 1986.

Articles

"Agape and Eros." Goshen, Ind.: Goshen College, 1956.

"Conflict in the Churches," *Harvard Divinity School Bulletin*, Winter, 1969.

"Does Anybody Love God?" Goshen, Ind.: Goshen College, 1956.

"How do We do Peace Theology?" *Essays on Peace Theology and Witness*. Elkhart, Ind.: Institute of Mennonite Studies, 1988.

"Love and Justice in Mennonite Mutual Aid." *The Compassionate Community*. Scottdale, Pa.: Association of Mennonite Aid Societies, 1970.

"The New Professional." *Harvard Divinity School Bulletin*, 1960.

"The Peace Churches as Communities of Discernment." *The Christian Century*. Vol. 80, September 1963.

"Preacher and Philosopher," *On Being the Church: Essays in Honor of John W. Snyder.* Peter C. Erb, ed. Kitchener, Ontario: Conrad Grebel Press, 1992.

"Prophetic Criticism and Corporate Responsibility." *Resource Packet on Civil Responsibility.* Newton, Kans.: Faith and Life Press, 1978.

"Rethinking Christian Life and Mission in Light of the Chinese Experience." *China and Christianity.* James D. Whitehead, Yu-Ming Shaw, N. J. Girardot, eds. Notre Dame, Ind., 1979.

About Pandora Press

Pandora Press is a small, independently owned press dedicated to making available modestly priced books that deal with Anabaptist, Mennonite, and Believers' Church topics, both historical and theological. Our books are typeset and printed using desktop technology. This allows us to produce short-run titles at a relatively low cost, while maintaining a high level of print quality. We welcome comments and suggestions from our readers.

Also Available from Pandora Press

C. Arnold Snyder, *Anabaptist History and Theology: An Introduction* (Kitchener, Ont.: Pandora Press, 1995). 434pp., 6 maps, 29 illustrations, softcover. ISBN 0-9698762-0-3
$35.00 U.S./$38.00 Canadian. Postage: $5.00 U.S./$6.00 Can.

C. Arnold Snyder, *Anabaptist History and Theology: Abridged Student Edition* (Kitchener, Ont.: Pandora Press, 1995). 268pp., 6 maps, 27 illustrations, softcover. ISBN 0-9698762-1-1
$25.00 U.S./$28.00 Canadian. Postage: $4.00 U.S./$5.00 Can.

C. Arnold Snyder, *The Life and Thought of Michael Sattler* (Scottdale, Pa.: Herald Press, 1984). 260pp., hardcover. ISBN 0-8361-1264-4
The author still has available some copies of this Herald Press book, now out of print. While supplies last.
$12.00 U.S./$14.00 Canadian. Postage: $4.00 U.S./$5.00 Can.

To order any of these books, or to receive information about upcoming titles, contact:

Pandora Press
51 Pandora Avenue N.
Kitchener, Ontario
Canada N2H 3C1 Telephone (519) 742-1876
e-mail casnyder@watserv1.uwaterloo.ca